TRAINING YOUR LOVE INTUITION

For Wise Relationship Choices

LeslieBeth Wish

ISBN: 978-1-7325284-1-3

TABLE OF CONTENTS

Dear Reader,

Learning how to make wise choices in love is one of the most important skills we need in life. But no matter how savvy we are about dating and mating, many of us have been duped in love.

Hmm…falling in love with someone who is a good match is not so easy, after all. And getting out of an unhealthy relationship quickly is not so easy either.

If the above paragraph sounds familiar, you probably asked yourself:

- How reliable is "chemistry" in the beginning?

- What's really wrong with sex soon?

- How do I know if my partner is good for me?

- Why did I miss the signs that this person was not good for me?

- Should I worry if we have disagreements? And what is the best way to resolve them?

And what does intuition have to do with all of these questions?

Research about love shows that trusting and training your intuition to be accurate is an essential component for finding an intimate partner who is good for you.

This book will help you answer all the questions above—and give you a guided program for training your love intuition to be accurate.

Who am I? I am LeslieBeth (LB) Wish, Ed.D, MSS, MA, a licensed psychotherapist, LCSW, and author who specializes in helping people become smart, brave, and intuitive about love, life, work, and happiness. My intuitive abilities developed early in life. And later in life, I was also trained by an internationally acclaimed teacher of intuition and other abilities. I write about things that worry me — especially when I can't explain them to myself and my clients. And when I can't explain things such as love relationships, I do research! You can trust that all the advice in this book is based on research with hundreds and hundreds of people.

I have created this unique, experiential book that I hope you will find deeply helpful in finding a good mate for you. Thank you for taking a look at this book. And thank yourself for already taking steps for emotional bravery! I wish you wisdom and happiness!

With Warmth & Support,
LB

What's In This Book?

Here are brief descriptions of the chapters:

FOUNDATIONS - Page 5 This part is the core of learning how to develop your intuitive assessments to be accurate — especially when it comes to love! Don't skip this part! In fact, you can apply the information in this chapter to other situations, such as your work environment! I repeat in some of the other chapters the charts and exercises that are in this chapter because you might choose to read first other sections or chapters that most apply to you—and because we know how aggravating it can be to hunt through a book to find important information!

READING PEOPLE - Page 23 If you can't read people — including reading YOU, then you put yourself at risk of being fooled. Yes, almost all of us have been fooled in love — including me! But the goals are to learn some tested and trusted people-reading skills that will help you choose an intimate partner more wisely — or help you get out of unhealthy relationships more quickly.

DATING - Page 41 What should you do on the first few dates? Is there such a thing as a "Soul Mate?" And if there is, why should that NOT be your best dating goal? And what about sex? When should you be sexually intimate? Learn in this chapter some surprising answers that come from research, counseling, and workshops with thousands of women and couples.

RELATING BETTER WITH YOUR PARTNER - Page 69 And even if you have made a wise love choice, you still need to fine-tune your relating skills. For example, what are the best ways to deal with differences? Learn some fun, tested, easy-to-do actions that can calm the situation, and that move you toward solution rather than stalemate.

SIGNS OF A GOOD AND BAD RELATIONSHIP - Page 87 Well, you've probably already heard too many times that "you have to work on your relationship," or that "no one is perfect." Even though both these thoughts are true, they don't always help you know whether your relationship is good or bad for you. This chapter will give you tested, trusted, research-based ways to see your relationship more clearly.

BREAK UPS - Page 113 Yes, sometimes it is wiser to break up. But just how do you know when to stop giving second, third — or even more chances? You will learn in this chapter about the most dangerous and the safest and wisest ways and reasons to breakup. And, of course, all the advice has been tested and tried.

Training Your Intuition to be Smart and Brave in Love
"THE ANSWER IS ALREADY IN YOU!"

Foundations

The power of intuition is in all of us! The secret is to know how to recognize it and trust it. Too often we sense that we should — or shouldn't — do something, but we override those messages.

Why do we do that? Read these sentences and then select the one choice that best describes how well the sentence applies to you.

QUIZ TIME!

1. I tend not to trust my judgment.

☐ Always True

☐ True

☐ Often True

☐ Sometimes True

☐ Rarely True

☐ Never True

2. I tend not to recognize my intuitive signal.

☐ Always True

☐ True

☐ Often True

☐ Sometimes True

☐ Rarely True

☐ Never True

3. When I do get that instinctive feeling, I tend not to listen to it.

- ☐ Always True
- ☐ True
- ☐ Often True
- ☐ Sometimes True
- ☐ Rarely True
- ☐ Never True

4. My parents / caregivers did not believe that I made good decisions.

- ☐ Always True
- ☐ True
- ☐ Often True
- ☐ Sometimes True
- ☐ Rarely True
- ☐ Never True

When I don't follow my intuition, it's because I dismiss it as unimportant or not really real.

- ☐ Always True
- ☐ True
- ☐ Often True
- ☐ Sometimes True
- ☐ Rarely True
- ☐ Never True

Save your answers. After you read this material, go back and look at your answers. This section will help you set the foundation for understanding, unlocking, and trusting your intuition. It includes explanations and exercises for you to do.

Let's start with some basic answers about intuition.

What Is Intuition?

Accurate intuition is a complex cognitive and physiological reaction to sensations and thoughts that originate from within you and from without you, and that prompts you to:

- Focus on what are the most important information and intuitive signals

- Exclude and not be distracted by other information

- Recognize the reaction to sensations as important

- Trust your reaction to be true—and then follow it!

Why Is Intuition Important?

Intuition is one of the cornerstones of sound decision-making in all aspects of your life. You might use other names for it such as "instinct" or "gut reaction." Often, without being aware that you are following your intuition, you have probably already used it to assess whether a person could be a good or unwise choice of friend or intimate partner.

And just in case you are not so sure whether intuition is real, think about this information:

- Nobel Prize Winner Daniel Kahneman discovered that we use intuition often in our life to make all kinds of decisions — large and small.

- Psychologists and authors John Kounios and Mark Beeman discovered that an area on the right side of the brain, just a bit above and behind the right ear, shows activity when you use your intuition!

So, now you know even more reasons that your accurate intuitive answers really are in you!

Imagine if you could develop a trained and trusted mindfulness so you could quickly detect, interpret, select,and accept as true the most valuable information about the cues and clues that come from you, around you and from other people.

Intuitive people are open people who accept that guidance can come from many sources. They know how to access more quickly and accurately all their powers. They don't separate feelings from thought or meaning. They use all their assessment powers.

Think about how Sherlock Holmes solved cases. He didn't just look for fingerprints. He saw a pattern that "connected the dots" between what, at first glance, seemed to be unimportant or un-detected clues. He trusted the interaction between his thoughts and feelings. In other words, he trusted his intuition.

What Are The Three Basic Steps To Empowering Your Intuition?

STEP 1: Sensing Your Sensations

Detecting cues, clues, and signs in you and others is the first step. Let's start recognizing your own unique way of receiving signals. For example, do you hear, see, think or feel your instincts and signs?

Like a good detective, look for patterns in your behavior in love, work, and other areas. Think of those maps on the wall on televisions shows where the detectives are studying the locations of crimes. They are looking for patterns that reveal clues about where the suspect lives or works.

Your pattern — or patterns — are unique to you. For example, you might sense your intuition differently, depending on whether you are making decisions in love, work, friendship or health. Most importantly, your physical, intuitive sign — or signs — are often as unique to you as your fingerprints!

But for now, focus on your love cues. Begin with this tested approach:

Detecting Your Love Intuition

A. Think back on a time when you received an intuitive sensation. Write some notes for each question.

A1. How did you receive the information? Was it a thought, a sound, a feeling, a vision?

A2. Did the sensation come from within you or without?

A3. Tell a brief story about an experience you had. Use the questions above as a guide.

A4. On a scale of 1-10, with 10 the highest, how would you rate the intensity of the sensation?

A5. On a scale of 1-10, with 10 the highest, how would you rate the duration of the sensation?

A6. On a scale of 1-10, with 10 the highest, how would you rate the frequency of the sensation?

A7. If you followed your intuition, what is it about you that made you follow it?

A8. If you did not follow your intuition, what is it about you that made you ignore or minimize it?

A9. Was your intuition correct — and should you have followed it?

B. Learn how to chart your intuition pattern.

Some people say that they make wiser decisions with their head (cognitive skills). Others say they use their heart (feelings). And some people say both. Here are two charts to help you recognize your various patterns.

B1. Think about your most recent or most troubling or confusing love situation. In each of the charts, think about the one place that describes you. Start with one scale, go to the other, and then think about that one place that includes both the horizontal and vertical scales.

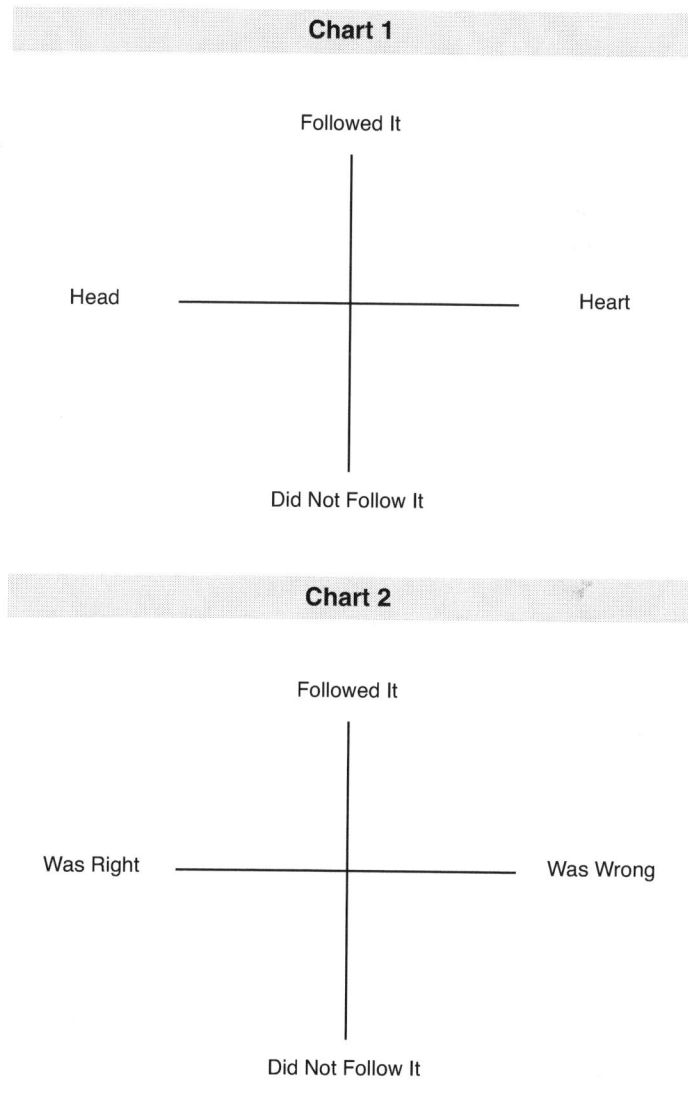

B2. What are you learning about you? Jot down your thoughts.

STEP 2: Trusting and Training Your Intuition

A. The act of trusting your intuition rests on being able to:

- STOP repeating behavior patterns that don't yield desired results

- STOP justifying decisions that are not good for you

- STOP listening to the maladaptive values, rules, and messages from your family

- STOP believing untrue family assessments of you

But these tasks are not easy. They require you to risk not being loved, accepted or approved of in your family. And since human beings' number one fear is abandonment, well, then, you can see why it seems wiser to toss out any awareness or use of cues and information that go against your family.

B. To trust your intuition, you must first recognize your caregivers' ways — and how you reacted to them.

Most likely, your family presented unwritten rules and role models that your caregivers told you about love, men, women, trust, anger and closeness. And even though these guidelines weren't posted on the refrigerator, you sort of absorbed them. These guidelines — whether you followed them or fought them — formed the emotional "country" that your family created.

And in this country of your family you developed your unique Emotional Default Drives — those thoughts, feelings, actions and reactions that you relied on to express your fears, feelings and needs.

These reactions just seem to "pop" out of you automatically!

Sometimes, your Emotional Default Drives consisted of behavior and values that *matched* your caregivers' ways and that *conformed* to their view of you — good or bad. And if they did, they probably allowed you to belong or even feel loved.

On the other hand, perhaps you developed your Emotional Default Drives in ways that *conflicted* with your caregivers' rules and ways. If so, then your Emotional Default Drives were likely attempts to fight your caregivers' values or negative views of you.

So, let's look at your unique Emotional Default Drives and the rules of your family's emotional country. Below are what my research revealed to be effective questions and statements to answer about you. Please select the words that describe you — *and add your own!*

B1.   In my family, I was the:

☐ maverick	☐ favorite	☐ an accident
☐ least favorite child	☐ Cinderella	☐ unwanted
☐ rebel	☐ forgotten	☐ pet or buddy
☐ fixer	☐ soother	
☐ dumb one	☐ smart one	
☐ good kid	☐ problem	

B2. In my family, I felt:

<table>
<tr><td>☐ loved</td><td>☐ stifled</td></tr>
<tr><td>☐ misunderstood</td><td>☐ mismatched</td></tr>
<tr><td>☐ taken for granted</td><td>☐ happy</td></tr>
<tr><td>☐ helped</td><td>☐ powerless</td></tr>
<tr><td>☐ trapped</td><td>☐ trusted</td></tr>
<tr><td>☐ sad</td><td>☐ picked on</td></tr>
<tr><td>☐ valued</td><td>☐ dismissed</td></tr>
</table>

B3. Which — if any of your answers — affect your ability to trust your intuition and judgment about you and your work?

B4. If friendly aliens had abducted you from your family when you were growing up, how would your family have changed?

For Example:

☐ Would they have fallen apart?
☐ Not missed you?
☐ Became depressed?
☐ Argued?
☐ Had another child?

What are you learning about your emotional role in your family? Think about how you recreate this role in your love relationships.

B5. Make a list of any of your negative self-talk thoughts or adjectives that go through your head about you.

For example:

- [ ] Bite off more than I can chew.
- [ ] Anxious
- [ ] Headstrong
- [ ] Pessimistic
- [ ] Not as smart as I think.
- [ ] Procrastinator
- [ ] Controlling
- [ ] Need to be too important.
- [ ] Unsure
- [ ] Argumentative

B6. List some of your family's sayings or beliefs.

Think about what they showed you about men, women, trust, anger or confidence.

For example:

- [ ] You're born, you live, you die.
- [ ] Show some respect for your father.
- [ ] We all put our pants on one leg at a time.
- [ ] Don't embarrass us.
- [ ] We want you to be your best.
- [ ] Work hard.
- [ ] The world doesn't owe you anything.
- [ ] Lots of luck going after your dream.
- [ ] Men just want one thing.
- [ ] The devil you know is better than the one you don't.
- [ ] Life is exciting and full of great things.
- [ ] Men are babies.

B7. List some of things your parents said to you about you—or to others about you.

For example:

☐ You gonna talk to us after you get your college degree?

☐ Make your grandpa proud.

☐ This one's got a mind of his / her own.

☐ Find what you like.

B8. Are there any matches between your answers to B5, B6 and B7?

Usually, we tend to carry around with us beliefs about **ourselves** that our parents had about **themselves**. That negative backpack could contain things such as your Emotional Default Drive and your doubts about trusting your judgment and decisions.

C. The goals of trusting your intuition are to:

- Free yourself from these restrictions so you can clear a path for trusting in your sensations and using them — even if you risk going against your family's ways

- Recognize when you are falling back on maladaptive beliefs, feelings and behavior

STEP 3: Using Your Intuition

A. Learning how to use and fine-tune your clues.

Here is an intuitive drill of the top three measurements to use. Rate them on a scale of 1-10, with ten the highest:

- How intense is the sensation?

- What is the duration of the sensation?

- What is the frequency of the sensation?

B. Answer these advanced questions:

- Would I characterize the sensation as positive or negative?

- To whom does the sensation apply?

- When do I sense the situation will occur?

- Is this a typical or trusted way for me to receive sensations?

- What action, if any, should I take now?

Congratulations! You are well on your way to training your intuition. Now you are ready to fine-tune your fine-tuning!

Exercise #1: Sensing the "YES or NO Feeling"

- Get some blank note cards, and write a different word on each: "Yes," "No," and "Maybe."

- Shuffle them and turn them face down.

- Now ask yourself a key question about whatever important issue or decision you are facing in your life right now. For example, are you struggling to decide whether to go out with someone for the first time? Or, whether to go out again with this person? Or, whether to be more physically intimate with this person? Or, whether not to date at all?

- Now turn over one of the cards. Read the answer out loud and then think it quietly to yourself. Read the answer out loud again and then think it quietly to yourself again.

- Notice your physical reaction. How does this card's answer make you feel? Now turn over another card and repeat steps C, D and E.

Turn over the last card and repeat steps C, D, and E. What are your learning about you?

Exercise #2: Meditation to Tap into Your Intuition

Many people have a difficult time meditating because they think they have to "shut their brain down." This is not necessarily true. The point of meditation is to simply quiet your mind a bit more so you can listen to your "inner voice."

It doesn't matter when or where you do your meditation, but it does matter that you are consistent and keep committed to doing it. And it can be short — just a couple of minutes — or as long as you want. Just do what feels right to you.

Do whatever works for you. Do you want to do it lying down in bed? Great. Do that. Do you want to sit upright in a chair? Do that. Whatever creates the most comfortable environment is what you should do. In order to quiet your mind, imagine relaxing powers flowing through your body. Count yourself "down" from 7 to 1 as many times as it takes to feel as though you are slowing down your brain waves.

Once you feel quieted, you might even find that you"hear" a voice that may or may not be your own. You might even start hearing messages in third person. The important thing to remember is to not QUESTION it. Just EXPERIENCE it. Feel it.

Once you practice meditation, it will come more naturally to you. And the more you do it, the more accurate answers will come to you.

Exercise #3: "Try On" Your Decision

This might sound like a strange thing to you. And you are probably even thinking, "Just how do I 'try on' a decision?"

Here's how.

You pretend to make a decision. For example, let's say you have two people who have asked you out. You went out with both, and you like each of them. But you know you have to choose one. What to do? Pretend that you already chose one. And keep pretending that you chose that person for at least a day or two.

Think about what your life would be like with that person. Visualize future scenarios in your head.

Now here's the really important part. Pay attention to your FEELINGS when you are visualizing. Do you generally feel good? If so, then it might be the right decision. Do you mostly feel bad? Then you are probably headed in the wrong direction.

Exercise #4: Let Others Make the Choice for You

Sometimes we can get into "analysis paralysis." In other words, we over-think to the maximum. When you over-think something, you edge out your intuition. Rational, logical thinking comes from a different part of your brain. But intuition comes from the emotional part of your brain. And remember, emotions aren't rational. They are feelings. And you can't argue with feelings.

When you find yourself in "analysis paralysis," stop. Literally, just stop thinking about it.

Then grab a few loved ones — people you really trust. Tell them you need to make this decision, but you're caught up in your over-analysis of the situation.

Now tell them that you want them to make the decision for you. They might look at you as if you're a bit crazy, but tell them that's what you want.

After they make the decision for you, pay attention to how it makes you feel. If it's the wrong decision, you will probably feel it. But you will also feel it if it's the right decision.

Ultimately, you are not going to really let others make the decision for you. The point of this exercise is to pay attention to your IMMEDIATE gut reaction to the other person's decision.

That will give you insight about the right answer that was evading you when you were in "analysis paralysis."

Exercise #5: Play Red-Light Green-Light in Your Head

Many people have played the "Red Light-Green Light" game as a child. But this time, you are going to play it with yourself … and all in your mind.

With your eyes open, think of a question you want an answer to. Then, close your eyes and immediately "see" a stoplight in your mind's eye.

What color is it? Red, green, or maybe even yellow? Again, don't over-think or over-see. If you don't see anything at first, that's fine. Don't get stressed out about it. Just trust. The goal here is to just eventually get your rational mind out of the way and look at the color you see in your head when you ask the questions.

Obviously, if you see green, that is equivalent to "yes" or "good." Red lights are negative. And Yellow lights are "caution."

The more you do this exercise, the better you will get at it.

Use this Foundation chapter as your base for re freshing, revising, and strengthening your accurate intuition!

AND DON'T FORGET TO THANK YOURSELF FOR YOUR EMOTIONAL BRAVERY.

Reading People

Getting Good at Reading People — Including Reading YOU
So You Can Be Wise and Happy in Love

Some people are instinctively great at reading people. They pick up on the smallest of non-verbal cues — and, most importantly, they know how to trust their intuition, interpret these cues, and take appropriate action.

For example, "Katy" was on a second date with "Glen" at a restaurant. On their first date they walked through the city park and talked about their interests. She was pleased to discover that they shared common activities. Yet, she detected a slight challenging tone in his voice.

But she agreed to go on a second date for a Sunday brunch. "I knew within the first five seconds of watching him eat that he was not good for me," she said. "He used his fork as a weapon, and he stabbed at his food and gobbled whole pieces." Her observation led her to envision Glen in a relationship as selfish, dismissive, critical, and potentially physically abusive.

How did Katy know all this?

Reading People Tip

She did what great people-readers do:
From small but telling behavior, she saw the
person's main character & issues.

Professional Poker Players call these observations "TELLS"

Katy wasn't wrong. By chance, when she volunteered to be on a community service committee, she met "Megan." They became friends, and Megan confided in her that she was very unhappy with her boyfriend Glen. Megan said Glen was critical, withdrawn and physically abusive.

Katy asked Megan to describe what Glen looked like and what he did for a profession. It was the same Glen!

Could you have sensed these warning signs from Glen's behavior?

Think back on your first few dates with a new person. What signs did you miss — or ignore?

Your Dating History Chart

- Write down the names of your previous, important intimate partners.

- Think about what "signs" you might have missed about their behavior. You know — the ones you ignored, minimized — or just plain didn't see!

- Write down these thoughts and observations.

- Write down your best guess as to why you didn't see these warning signs before. Hints: Ask yourself:

- What was going on in my life that made me choose or fall in love at that time?

- What was it about this person that I liked or believed he or she was The One?

- How surprised am I that I chose this kind of person — and acted the way I did with him or her?

- What factors from my upbringing might have influenced — or blinded me?

Reading People Tip

Relationship research continues to show that non-verbal cues, including tone of voice, are better indicators of potential problems.

So, how can you get good at reading people? You need to learn:
Intuition Matters

- Recognize the basics of reading body language

- Detect your own physical and mental reactions

- Trust your intuitive judgment—and follow it!

- Change your dating goal from finding The One to testing whether your observations and intuitive assessment are correct.

Don't worry if you are not good at doing these tips. Detecting and trusting the signs of body language take practice. Here's a great list to help you with one of love's biggest issues: *Is This Person Telling the Truth?*

Recognizing the Basics of Reading Body Language:

Reading the Body Language of Liars.

80-90% of the meaning of a message is contained in the non-verbal portion of it. In other words, it's not what you say, but it's how you say it.

Body language communicates our attitudes and feelings—and it's often unconscious. Our unconscious behavior is often the most truthful. So that's why it's important to learn the signs of lying and other untruthful behavior.

Sometimes our conscious mind may not pick up on these signs, but the more you know about them, the better you will get at deciphering the good and bad signs in someone before you ever enter into a relationship with them.

According to research, here are some major signs of lying behavior:

- Covering the mouth

- Placing an object between yourself and the other person (as "protection")

- Sudden crossing of legs

- Sudden crossing of arms

- Glancing away / sideways

- Forced, unnatural eye contact

- Overly stiff posture

- Clenching

- Fidgeting

- Hiding the hands

- Pupil contraction

- Controlled vocal tone

- Stutters, slurs, or hesitations

- Sweating

- Sudden giggling

- Lack of eye contact

Reading Normal-Enough Body Language

Okay, we all miss some cues that would have helped us read someone more accurately. But, in general, it is your responsibility to sharpen your observational skills. Here is a brief list of things to observe:

- How patient is your date when you linger, take too long to order, change your mind, change plans, and other similar, everyday situations? Impatience at small things might be a "tell" about your date's ability to handle big things!

- How much does your date try to impress you? Does your date take over the discussion? Order for you? Show off knowledge of wine and food? Act like he or she is "an important regular at the restaurant?" Make all the decisions about where and what you will be doing?

• Does your date touch you too much in the beginning?

• Does your date lean in too close — or lean back too far?

• Does your date talk too much about themselves — or not reveal much at all about themselves?

• Does your date have dirty or bitten fingernails?

• Does your date flirt — or act rudely with the wait staff ?

• Does your date offer you a taste of his or her dish?

• Does your date plan everything about the evening — and seem to mock you if you don't want to go back to each other's places?

• Do you have — but brush aside — any negative observations of your date?

• Would you want your friends or family members to date this person? Would they object — and if so, why?

Some "Starter" Thoughts about Detecting Your Own Physical and Mental Reactions

Observing someone else is only the beginning of getting good at training your intuition in reading people.

You also must learn to read YOU! Too often, we fail to detect our own reactions. And, even worse, when we do, we tend to ignore or minimize them! Oops!

Why do we ignore these signals? In general, it is because we want to feel emotionally comfortable and right!

And why do we want to? Go back to your Dating History and think more in depth about why you placed so much importance on the date that you missed or minimized important clues.

For example, were you activating your caregivers' rules, values or view of you? Were you relying on "chemistry" to tell you that this person was The One?

Obviously, your most important tool in reading people is reading — and knowing YOU!

Begin with Detecting Your Body's Reactions

So, when you are on your dates, observe your physical reactions and thoughts. Is your tummy doing flip-flops? And is it doing that as a warning sign — or a sign of your being happy and right about this person? Hmmm…how confusing!

You can also take a break, go into the bathroom, and do a "feeling and thought" check. Begin with your head and work your way down your body.

Ask yourself:

- Just what am I feeling? Where am I feeling it? Have I felt that feeling before? If so, what did I learn from it? Did those feelings help me make a wise — or unwise choice of partner?

- What thoughts about my reaction — or my date — are going through my head? Are they positive or negative?

- Who — or what does this person remind me of? I often coach people to think of an animal — or especially a dog breed — that most reminds you of your date.

- How does this person fit into my usual choices of partners? Is that good or bad?

- What do I predict he or she will do and say on another date?

Change your dating goal from finding The One to testing whether your observations and intuitive assessment are correct.

Reading People Tip

The more you date, the better you get at reading others.
If you "hide out" and avoid the chance of love,
you will weaken your people-reading skills!

So, most of the time, go out on that second date to confirm, tweak or change your assessment.

And, most importantly: *Forget about "chemistry" in the very beginning!* Think back on all the other times when you:

- Felt "chemistry" with someone

- Assumed it meant that you met The One

- And then, oops! That person turned out to be

- The Wrong One!

Research in long-term, mutually happy couples report that a high number of these couples said they did not feel that instant chemistry in the beginning!

Think about romantic comedies where the two people do not start out liking each other! You, the viewer, know they will get together — but it takes a while!

And, often in these romantic movies, one of the persons thinks he or she is in love with someone else — but you, the viewer, know that the person is wrong!

Is there such a thing as love at first sight — with a good match? YES!!! But first you must trust your assessment of you and your people-reading skills.

Know Your Present Emotional Situation

- People who choose wisely instantly know their current vulnerabilities. The most common ones that can blind you to reading a person accurately include:

- Getting older — and feeling desperate to find anyone who is "good enough"

- Feeling your "biological clock" ticking

- Feeling lonely or sorry for yourself

- Feeling upset about being the only sibling or cousin who isn't married or living with someone

- Feeling frightened by life and needing to have a partner

- Experiencing a trauma

- Experiencing a loss of a loved one, home or job

- Getting diagnosed with a serious disease

All the things on the list above can:

- Weaken your ability to detect your intuitive, physical reactions

- Prevent you from reading the signals accurately

- Impede your ability to believe in the accurate signals

- Prevent you from taking action!

Trust Your Intuitive Judgment—and Follow It!

Reading People Tip

The better you get at reading people, the more you
develop trust in your intuitive assessments —
and the more you learn about YOU!

Now that you have a better understanding of how you get in the way of reading people accurately, here are some more in-depth exercises.

Ask yourself the following questions. I strongly recommend that you do one or more of the following:

- Talk your answers out loud to yourself

- Make a recording of yourself answering each question

- Talk out your answers and thoughts to a trusted friend or family member or professional person

- Keep a journal of your ideas and your dating experiences.

Over time, review your answers. See what you are learning. Notice what you still need to learn, change, and triumph over!

Questions to Fortify Your Intuitive People-Reading Skills

- Am I too excited about this person—and am I allowing my excitement to cloud my people- reading skills?

- Am I going back and forth between people who are too mean or meek?

- Am I relying on "instant chemistry" to determine if this person is right for me?

- Am I eliminating this person because of one thing that is not important to me?

- Am I ignoring my intuitive signals from my body and my thoughts in my head that say that this person is not good for me?

- Do I have a "love checklist" that involves superficial things?

- Do I know my emotional state at the moment — and can I sense if I am choosing or not choosing a partner in reaction to my emotional state?

- Review these questions several times. Look at them again before you go on your dates!

The MOST Powerful Questions to Help You Get Rid of What Gets in Your Way of Reading People Accurately

In this chapter, you might have noticed that I asked you a few questions about your upbringing. You might have thought: "oh no — psychobabble."

Or: "How could my upbringing possibly affect my ability to read people accurately?

The quick answers are: It does — because you always carry your past with you wherever you go and whatever you do, not do, think, feel — *and detect and therefore "read" in others.*

Your caregivers influence how you regard you! They contribute to your confidence, competence, and self-esteem. And you base your view of you on how they treat you and what they say to you.

And you either accept or reject their view of you.

But, in truth, it's not easy to see yourself differently. It takes great inner strength. Why, you might think. Why should it be so difficult to say to your young self: "Well, that's their idea of me. Not mine."

In addition, your sibling profile also profoundly shapes you. But before you get trapped in what you might have learned about your birth order and sibling profile, let's do an important change to those concepts.

Yes, it's essentially true that your sibling profile and birth order are key elements in shaping your character, but they aren't fixed. For example, the oldest sisters of sisters, or the oldest brother of brothers sometimes are not the serious and often bossy, insensitive ones — who are usually the favorite or most relied-upon one in the family.

And, the younger sister of a brother, or the younger brother of a sister do not always choose as an intimate partner someone who is an older sibling.

Why not? Because it can happen in families that the oldest is not the most responsible, take charge person — or that the youngest person is not the follower. And this situation occurs because there can be random genetic changes about health, intelligence, abilities, mood, leadership, and anxiety levels that do not conform to the theory of birth order and sibling profiles.

Think about you and your siblings. Who is the responsible one?

The kind one? The baby? The forgotten one?

Let's use the story of "Irene" as an example.

Irene's Story

Irene is the oldest sister of a sister and two brothers. Her charming, dynamic but flawed father drank a lot, and often came home from his job as a salesman tired and cranky. It was not unusual for him to drink too much.

On weekends, when he said he needed "to relax," he often got so drunk that Irene had to fetch him from the neighborhood bar. Irene's mother was busy tending to the younger children. Irene became the responsible one.

And just what kind of men did she choose for partners? Men who drank or men who needed her to take charge. She had emotional radar for charming, handsome but weak, ineffective men.

When she met a man who was not a drinker or who was effective and competent in life, she felt that she wasn't needed or valued. She felt comfortable with men who needed fixing because it was a familiar pattern for her. Besides, she secretly wondered what a healthy man would see in her — and, even worse, how would she *keep* him?

So, it is no surprise that Irene misread some important signs in her men. For example, if they drank too much, she figured it was manageable. If they were not reliable and showed up late or didn't have enough money in their wallet, she just thought: "That's men for ya'!" (Words her mother said all the time!)

And if the man did not drink or did not need a woman to take over, Irene's assessment of them was that they were boring, not charming, not challenging — and just plain too ordinary.

I hope you are beginning to see how easy it is for your family history to intrude on your people reading skills.

And so, like Irene in our story above, you risk developing emotional comfort with the familiar — even if the familiar is not good for you.

As a result, in your dating choices, you tend to reproduce relationship patterns that fit with your emotional comfort zone of "you in your family's upbringing of you."

Breaking that pattern can cause tremendous anxiety. You can feel that you are indeed in strange and unknown emotional waters. You don't really know how to act, how not to take the lead all the time. Just how are you supposed to act? "What does he see in me?" you wonder.

Irene did meet a man who was good for her. And, this time, she tried to stay with him. But she felt intense anxiety. She had nightmares of being left alone in a jungle.

Her anxiety got so out of control that she asked her doctor for medication. He referred her to a psychiatrist who wisely asked her about her, "What would happen if you were not there in your family?'

Irene was shocked at what came out of her mouth. She said, "My family would have fallen apart — and my Dad would have gotten worse. And my poor mother would collapse from all the stress."

The psychiatrist said, "How terrifying." And then he asked her, "And what else are you afraid of?"

The answer shocked her. She thought she would say something about her insecurity about the relationship. Instead she said: "He isn't anything like the men in my family. Bringing him home to meet my parents would make them feel small and wrong — and they might not want me to return if I am with him."

Irene's story is a great example of the deep fears of reading people accurately and risking bucking the family system. Human's greatest fear — rational or not — is being abandoned — even if you are all grown up and don't need to rely on your family any longer!

How unfair! But that is how we humans get made. But you can alter those family messages and ways!

And a great place to start is to free up your ability and self-permission to read people accurately.

And Here are the MOST Powerful Questions to Ask Yourself

Ta-da!

Now that you can see the connection between your past and your intuitive skills in reading people, start a journal so you can answer the following questions. You might need to revise your answers as you learn more about your unhealthy comfort levels and your choice of dates.

- Am I falling into dating and relating patterns that reproduce unhealthy ways that I was treated or talked to in my family of origin?

- Am I afraid to date someone who is really different from my previous choices of partner?

- Am I afraid to date someone who — in a healthy way — does not "fit" into my family of origin?

- Or am I choosing an unhealthy choice of partner because he or she does fit into my family's style, problems, and shortcomings?

- What cues have I missed on my previous dates and relationships?

The next time you go on a date or meet someone, be sure to keep these questions in mind!

Keep your emotional door open to meeting new people! Practice "Regret Management." Would you really want to:

- **Regret missing the opportunity to find a good match for you?**

- **Regret not getting emotionally brave enough to learn about you — and miss out on healthy love?**

YOU CAN TOUGH OUT LOVE MISSTEPS!

Dating

Well, you probably already know that dating can really feel as though you are "going out on a limb" sometimes. So, it's no surprise that smart dating especially requires trusting your intuition. Think of the times you thought someone was a potential match — and then felt blindsided when he or she revealed that "hidden" self.

You can't predict suitability in every person. Some people are really good at presenting a false self. For an extreme example, think of the true crime television shows where the killer was a respected, accomplished, and charming person.

Dating is both exciting and scary — and sometimes it is difficult to tell which emotion you are feeling about your date or new love!

Why? Well, look at what's at stake — your greatest fear: that you made a mistake! OUCH. And we all know that no matter how smart we are to get out of a bad relationship, the feelings and thoughts we have about misreading our partner linger — and confuse us.

This chapter will help you take a look at your interactions with your partner, and teach you about how relationships work, and answer your most nagging questions!

Let's start with a brief dating quiz. You can test your ideas against the findings from research. Read each question and the choice of answers. Which answer would you choose?

QUIZ TIME!

1. What is women's most common serious love issue?

A. Having extra marital affairs

B. Experiencing domestic violence

C. "Swearing off intimate partners — and love" for a prolonged time after being "fooled" or breaking up

Discussion:

The studies about how many women have extra marital affairs vary. Duh — of course, they do! How honest would you be on a survey where the researcher might be able to identify you?

Yet, the more anonymously women can answer this question, the more reliable the answer. The overall findings of well-constructed research indicate about a quarter to almost a third of women report having extra marital affairs.

But don't panic if you are having—or had an affair. Solid research also shows that about a third of couples who experience affairs stay together and heal.

Let's look at the next choice about domestic violence.

The 2011 United Nations' Women Study of the prevalence of domestic violence of women in 86 countries reveals that 70% of women report physical and sexual abuse in their lifetime by a husband or intimate partner.

And here's the last choice about "swearing off men, partners, and love."

My core study of over 1,200 women, plus the findings of noted marital experts such as Dr. John N. Gottman, shows that 70% women, after being emotionally hurt in love, "swear off intimate partners and love" for the most common range of time of 6-9 months to more than five years.

If you chose B or C, about domestic violence or swearing off love, you are correct.

You can lessen your tolerance for domestic violence by:

- Seeking professional help immediately

- Developing a safety plan with a professional as soon as you feel unsafe, threatened or harmed

- Establishing economic ability to support you.

The danger of swearing off love is less dramatic but still potentially harmful to you emotionally and physically. The top dangers of swearing off partners and love are:

- You get rusty about reading your emotional, mental, behavioral, and physiological cues in you and partners about potential abusers — or just not good matches in a partner for you

- You perpetuate a negative attitude about you and love. This negativity can lead you to accept mistreatment when you do start dating again

- Your isolation leaves you vulnerable to the hurt-lonely-scared-and-grab the next person who comes along cycle if you experience a crisis

And what about men and their worst fears about love?

The answers are similar:

- Making an unwise choice of partner

- Staying with an unwise choice of partner.

2. What attracts women the most in a partner?

A. An exciting person

B. Someone just like her

C. A mild person

Discussion:

The research of anthropologists such as Dr. Helen Fisher, and of marriage therapists such as Dr. John N. Gottman show that women are attracted to partners who are providers. They theorize that, regardless of women's ability to take care of themselves financially and emotionally they are still attracted to partners who demonstrate success.

Exciting partners are often the ones who are good providers. No surprise there — they tend to be successful, dynamic, and savvy about the world. But be careful! This person's sense of authority in life can easily morph in to a sign of authoritarianism and control over you! My research also showed that women prefer exciting and dynamic partners.

Let's look at the next choice: Someone just like you!

Yes, it's true that sharing common values and backgrounds such as religious beliefs can be an important part of mutual happiness. However, it is differences in strengths and problem-solving styles that can create stronger bonds and coping abilities. Couples not only can learn from each other, but they can also form a powerful, problem-solving team where they each bring a different perspective.

And now let's look at the last choice about easy-going partners.

We often like people who are easy-going, but sometimes these are the people who are more likely to avoid confrontation and tough situations.

The answer is A — an exciting person.

If you choose an exciting person, become observant of signs of controlling behavior. For example, does your partner often do any of the following behaviors?

- Criticize you — especially in public

- Discount your opinions or needs

- Isolate you from your family or friends

- Withhold affection, emotions or discussions about problem-solutions

- Disallow you to have your own checkbook.

And what about what attracts men?

Men's issues are similar to women's. And, yes, it is still true that men tend to be more visual than women. As a result, they tend to be more attracted to a partner who visually pleases them.

But that potential partner does not necessarily have to be beautiful or handsome. In fact, studies show that in bars, men do not approach the most physically attractive people out of fear of being rejected!

3. What is women's most common fear about falling in love?

A. The person later wants you to change lifestyles and professions

B. Women cannot trust their own judgment about people

C. The parents of one or both won't approve of the choice of partner

Discussion:

Life cannot be totally planned. There are unforeseen surprises and forks in the road. For example, many students in college or trade schools end up surprised that they changed their majors and areas of concentration.

However, couples who *nurture each other's growth* find ways to support and incorporate these alterations.

Let's look at the next choice about trusting your judgment.

One of the keys to selecting a wise choice of partner is the ability to read and assess your partner correctly. However, reading another person accurately depends on your skills in mindfulness. You need to detect and interpret your emotional, physiological, behavioral, and mental reactions when you are with your partner.

Developing the skills about really knowing you requires a very high degree of emotional bravery. You have to be able to withstand honest, psychological self-examination. If you can't tough out your disappointment and confusion about you, then you risk choosing partners who repeat your old and not very wise dating patterns. And then guess what happens? You got it — you mistrust your judgment even more! *People who tolerate the anguish of self-knowledge make better choices of partners.*

And now let's look at the last choice of parental disapproval.

Parental rejection hurts. But sometimes your parents' values, beliefs, and lifestyles might not be healthy. Being different from your parents might be a good idea. Wisdom is based on knowing whether to choose a partner who is similar or different to your family.

The correct answer is B—about trust or not trusting your judgment.

And what about men?

They do, too, struggle whether to trust or not trust their judgment. How did you do?

Well, now you're primed and ready to challenge your thinking about dating! Let's start with the beginning stages of dating.

I.
In The Beginning: Your Top Issues, Questions, And Answers

A. What is Your Dating Mindset?

Read the following statements. Which statement(s) applies to you?

1. I believe a person can fall in love at first sight.

2. I believe "that if it (love) is meant to be, it will just happen."

3. Love happens when you're not looking for it.

Can you guess which belief or beliefs is not healthy for you?

It is true that a person can fall in love "at first sight." Well, the statement doesn't exactly mean the very moment that you see someone. But it does apply to meeting someone, spending a bit of time with them, observing them — and then sensing that this person is a really good love choice for you.

You might meet at a party or on a first date. But, regardless of how you meet, you both just "click." So, what is the secret to falling in love right away? Here is the best magic formula:

You know the dating patterns to avoid

- *You are good at reading people.*

- *You have a positive mindset and an open heart about love.*

- *You are in a good place in your life.*

But is it true that love can just "happen?" Not really. Okay, yes, there is the aspect of luck. But then you have to be emotionally prepared to take advantage of that luck — and that means having all the items on the list above about how to fall in love at first sight.
Besides, do you really think the universe is going to tilt toward you — even if you do nothing emotionally or behaviorally to prepare for this gift?

Okay, what about love happening when you are not looking for it. Hmmm…well, that can kind of be an accurate statement. How? Well, if you have all those qualities in the list above, then you can find love when — and where you least expect it — and are not desperate for it. Your emotional maturity, self-honesty, and your healthy state of mind and heart are in a good, calm, and wise place.

B. What do you think about when—and if—you should have sex?

Read the following statements. Which statement(s) applies to you?

1. If I like the person, I don't see why we shouldn't have sex on the first date.

2. If I regret having sex with someone, then I think it's best to end any contact.

3. I don't know how long it is advisable before having sex with someone I like.

4. If we don't "click" sexually right away, then I don't think the person would make a good match for me.

Can you guess which belief or beliefs are not healthy for you?

Read the following section, **Let's Talk SEX**, for the answers!

Let's Talk SEX

So, what's really wrong with sex on the first date? The reasons are not about ethics, morals, or even your religious beliefs.

The question of when to have sex is about you being in charge of your life.

Think about this question: Would you make an important decision in your life while you were drunk? Hopefully not!

Well, when your pleasure hormones from sex get aroused, your brain is hijacked! You feel great, high, special, invincible—alive!! WOWEE!!

But do you know what is not alive: Your judgment. And do you know what is alive—and very aroused:

Your need to attach to this person with whom you just had sex. Why?

Your aroused hormones include oxytocin — that's right —that's the same hormone that intensify the connection between a mother and her child — during and after pregnancy!

And for men after highly satisfying sex they can also feel a strong attachment. Their pleasure hormones, their sense of sexual confidence, and the specific things going on in their lives such as loneliness or getting older can boost their feelings of falling in love.

So, what do you really risk having after sex with someone you hardly know? You have:

- An urge and longing to get attached to a stranger

- A tendency to justify your behavior by the fact that you now feel this urge and longing

- An experience of a not-so-wise way of masking your loneliness and anxieties

- Oops!

But if you do regret having sex with someone, is there any going back? Dealing with "sexregret" can eat away at your sense of control over your life. But don't beat yourself up about it — especially if you like your date.

If you would like to see the person again—but you don't want it to lead to sex, tell your new person:

- I really like you!

- I enjoyed having sex with you very much.

- And already I find myself liking, respecting, and caring about you.

- Let's just slow down and get to know each other better before we have sex again.

And guess what? Very few people would pass up that opportunity to be valued and loved!

So, let's say you didn't have sex right away. Just when should you have sex? Of course, there is no simple answer to that question, but here are questions to ask yourself:

- Do we like and respect each other?

- Do I have any of those nagging doubts in my head that I would like to ignore?

- Do we regard each other as friends,too?

- Have we confided personal things about ourselves to each other? Do we enjoy just "hanging out"together?

- Is it easy to be with friends?

- Do we "get" each other?

- Do we share common values?

But what if you do have sex and it's not good? For women, especially, find those positions and love-making styles that work for you. Don't give up on your new partner if you don't feel that high and rush after sex.

A mutually happy sex life can take time. Play "School for Sex" where you each take turns being the pupil and the teacher.

Time is your best friend. Wait to see if your partner reveals that they have sex problems. Find out if these issues can easily be remedied — or are they signs of deeper and worrisome problems.

However, if your partner wants you to do things that make you uncomfortable or afraid, well, don't do it. And seriously consider never seeing this person again if the sex acts involve fear and disrespect.

C. How do I fix a bad first impression and other "goof ups?"

Read the following statements. Which statement(s) applies to you?

1. If I "mess up" a date somehow, I feel so embarrassed that I think it is best not to see the person again.

2. When I sense that I've made a bad first impression, I like texting the person an explanation because it seems less anxiety-provoking than talking.

3. I take a look at my behavior and understand it — and then I send emoji and other texts and even phone calls asking for a second chance.

Can you guess which choices are not healthy for you?

We all have had experiences where we would like a "re-do." And having one on a date does not mean you should avoid your date. Don't deprive yourself of an opportunity to see if the person will give you a second chance. If the person doesn't give you that chance, take a sigh of relief. You don't want someone who isn't an understanding and flexible person!

But, please don't send a text for that second chance! Be real.

Don't add emotional remoteness just to protect yourself from you —and, as discussed above—from observing the kindness or lack of empathy from your date.

And certainly don't beg or overwhelm your date with numerous pleas! You will look desperate.

So, what should you do?

Call your date and leave a message that you have something very sweet to tell them — but that you don't just want to leave an ordinary message.

And here is your message:

Hello, (date's name). This message is a Product Recall for (your name), who (briefly fill in the blank.) (Here are typical choices:)

- Spoke out of turn

- Had a very bad day

- Acted hastily

- Was not themselves due to (fill in the blank)

(Your name) is now asking you to please try out (your name) again because (she or he) really liked and respected you — and thinks you might have some important things in common.

Thank you, The Management of (your name)

What if there is no "chemistry" on the first date?

Do you believe: "No chemistry — no second date!"

There certainly are some horrible and even terrifying dates that you do not need to repeat! One of the women in my study said that the man brought pornographic cartoons with him on the date to show her at dinner!

Another woman said that the man spent the date making sarcastic statements about her lack of knowledge about fine dining. He even said to her: "I thought you were sophisticated. What did you do—fall off the cabbage wagon?"

But what if there just is no reason to nix the date other than the issue of "chemistry?"

What?? Have you forgotten already about romantic comedies? Almost always each person does not like or get along with the other. And then — BOOM!! — they really get rid of their biases, get over their own hang ups, and finally "see" each other as a good match!

So, what should you do?

1. Think about all those times when you wanted a "second chance."

2. Think back on all those times you were wrong in your assessment of someone!

3. Subscribe to the "Baseball Theory of Dates." Batters get

three chances to strike out. Give your date at least one chance to make a better connection!

II.
The Next Few Dates: Your Top Issues, Questions, And Answers

Got one of those Dating Checklists?

Having one isn't a bad thing. It all depends on how you use it!

Select only one choice from each statement about Dating Checklists

A. Checklists are like emotional insurance policies against making another bad choice of partner.

B. Checklists only help if you have the right kind of things on them.

C. Your date should have more than half the things on the checklist.

The answer is B. Why?

Too often people use detailed dating checklists as a shield—and a self-lie. You can then say to yourself:

"Well, I never turn down getting fixed up. I always talk to people who interest me. I make myself talk to people I don't know at parties. I accept dates — but none of them have exactly what I want."

Because your checklist has so much on it, no one can possibly fulfill your items. And so, you can go to sleep at night believing that you really"tried."

And what do you get out of that? Well, you can end up protecting yourself from your fears of making another wrong choice, and of being rejected and *known* to your partner and you!

Huh? What do we mean by being "known?" Well, love requires emotional bravery — which is one of the hardest tasks of the self. Accepting and knowing YOU take depth and inner strength.

> We all have weaknesses, we all have made mistakes, and we all have limitations. Your love intuition weakens when you cannot know and accept these shortcomings. As a result, you risk never finding or making a good choice of partner because you don't believe you are good enough for healthy love.

So, what kind of things should be on a checklist? And how many items should my potential partner have from the list?

You can make lists of lots of things that are important to you. And you can mark the ones that are the most important. And you can also create those Plus and Minus charts about your new dates.

Those ideas are not bad advice at all, but think back on your previous experiences about pluses and minuses for other decisions you've made, such as which apartment or job to take. You probably read your charts a few times — and then you just (sort of) made a decision — and hoped it was right.

And if it were right, your intuition probably guided you. And, if you were really smart, you discovered that some important items got left out — and you still felt as though you made a good choice.

Wise love can be like that, too. We don't tend to get everything — but we get enough of the top things.

And what are those top things to consider on our checklist?

Everyone's list is unique, but here are the top things that emerged from my findings. Tweak or add your own.

The Beginnings of a Dating Checklist

1. We like and respect each other.

2. I like who and how I am in this relationship.

3. We are a good team because we bring complementary skills to the relationship.

4. We are good problem-solvers.

5. We don't rely on arguing, criticizing, or avoiding issues.

6. We share common values.

7. We have fun and laugh.

8. Our time together is easy.

9. I do not overlook, minimize, excuse, or "explain away" my serious doubts.

10. I am getting my unique needs met.

Good—but what does number 10 mean?

BINGO! That is where your deepest homework about YOU comes in. The best choices of partners are people who are able to "correct" for your past hurts that you experienced in your family — without "over-correcting" so much that you are robbed of personal growth.

Think about these brief, true scenarios of good partners.

"Melanie" was the youngest of four sisters. She was always called "The Baby." Everyone took care of her. She grew up believing that she was incapable in life. She married "Bob" who took over everything — and eventually controlled her.

She broke up with "Bob," did some soul-searching, and then met "Paul." Paul was an older brother of sisters, and he seemed to have a natural understanding of women. He was a benevolent leader who also helped his partner feel confident. They have been happily married for decades.

"Samantha" was the oldest of brothers and sisters. She just always ended up making decisions. She dated "Burt" for years, but the more successful she became, the less she respected him.

She had an affair with "Tim," who was capable without being bossy or controlling. She was ashamed of herself for cheating on "Burt," and she finally left him. She knew "Tim" was a better match. She realized about herself that she actually felt "lonely at the top." She was exhausted from shouldering all the relationship responsibilities.

Yet, her childhood taught her the importance of "doing everything yourself." She thought she had to do everything so that nothing could go wrong. Oh no, she thought. She had turned into an impossible perfectionist — just like her mother.

Samantha vowed that she would learn to tough out the anxiety of handing over some of the responsibility to a partner. The trick was to find that person. Luckily for her, "Tim" was a good match.

YOU in DEPTH: A Worthwhile Review of YOU!

Write down in a journal or on a piece of paper all the sayings — positive and negative — that your parents said about you, life, unhappiness, fairness, love, men, and women.

On a separate page or piece of paper, write down all the things about you that you don't like, that you are afraid to let someone know about you, and the things that you did that you aren't proud of when you were in other relationships.

Now look at each list carefully. Do you see similarities between what your parents did or said and what you wrote on your list about you?

So, how do you get out of you what's inside you that you don't like?

1. Tell yourself that your parents' actions and words tell you about them and their issues — and not necessarily you.

2. Understand and face that these issues that you have absorbed can be what attracts you to a partner who re-creates a familiar but unhealthy relationship pattern.

3. Now tell yourself that you can become more aware of your pattern and choice tendencies.

4. Accept that you will feel uncomfortable when you are not re-creating those patterns.

5. Tough out the discomfort so you can have greater freedom in choosing a good match!

For example, "Rhonda," one of the women in the study said that her mother always made snide remarks about her being athletic and competitive in sports. Her mother said things such as: "Men don't like muscular women. You have to let men win."

Rhonda didn't even know that she had incorporated these beliefs when she was growing up. Looking back, she realized that she always ended up falling for men who were also athletic, competitive — and abusive!

And so, she *over-corrected* that bad choice and chose men who were too passive, and who wanted her to be in charge. She felt so alone after awhile.

Buried deep within her was a belief that no sane man would want a woman like her. And then she met "Charlie." She finally found a partner who respected and valued the athlete in her!

Why do I flip back and forth between partners who are too mean or too meek?

Avoiding The Flip Cycle

It's easy to get stuck in a Flip Cycle of Love Patterns. You hope someone very different is the solution. For example, let's say you tend to be attracted to someone who seems to be a successful and charismatic leader. Those qualities are very admirable. No wonder you like his or her confidence and success.

But, oh no, you misread this appeal. This person actually wants to lead you by the nose. He or she dismisses your needs and requests. Their career and other interests come first. And then, sometimes, this person leads with his or her fists.

So, you break up finally, and you vow to choose someone who has a mild manner. There is nothing wrong with a loving, even-tempered person who wants to be close to you. Yet, later you discover that this partner often can't be decisive.

So, you say to yourself: "No more baby-people." And then you over-correct again, and you choose someone whose pattern is to take charge of life — and then of you.

Or, perhaps you were in a relationship where you were "two peas in a pod" and did everything together. But, oops! And although this person was sweet, their attentiveness turned into suffocation. The air seemed to go out of your personal time.

So, you say to yourself: "I got to find someone who doesn't need me so much." And then you over-correct and choose someone whose pattern is to do their own thing so much that you feel alone.

But notice that these examples are just upside-down versions of the same pattern where someone is either too much or too little in charge or too passive, clingy, or controlling.

The healthiest relationships consist of partners who fill in the gaps for the other partner's weaknesses and who can offer these important qualities:

- Flexibility

- Reliability

- Balanced Closeness and Togetherness (Feeling Warmth but also Independence)

- Balanced "Say" in a Relationship (Feeling Safe but also Independent but not Controlling)

- Complementary Strength

Now you can see why paying attention to your interactions is more important than worrying about "types" of people.

Here is a chart that you might have seen before in this book. This chart is so important that I feature it — and other information — several times to make key points. Besides, truly grasping and applying all the concepts in this book require repetition. And it's aggravating in books when you want to flip to particular points — and can't find them in. So, I decided to include them again, briefly, to help you learn more easily.

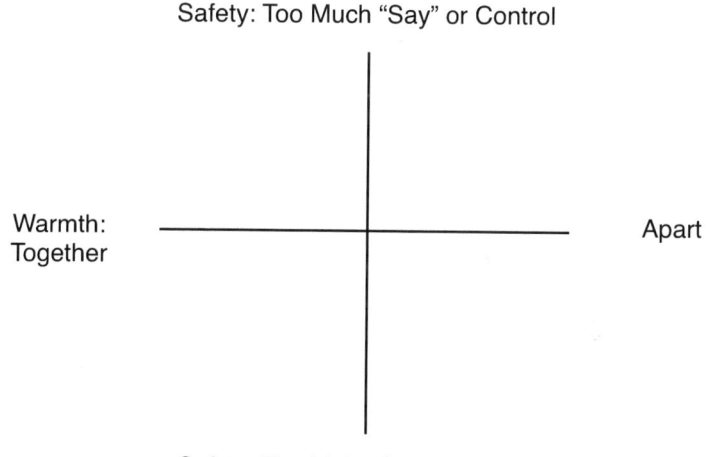

The "Bones" of Love

Safety: Too Much "Say" or Control

Warmth: Together

Apart

Safety: Too Little "Say" or Control

Why should I change my dating goal from "Finding the One" to Reading People?

Remember — the main goal is to build trust in your intuitive judgment. And as you might have learned in other chapters, we advise you to go out again with a date to test whether your assessment is accurate. You can always say no to more dates later.

What are the best dates?

Make your date resemble real life! Bring along your friends. Run errands together! Most of life in a long-term relationship is spent doing very ordinary things!

What questions should I ask after a few dates if I am really interested in this person?

- What have you learned about you from your previous relationships?

- Tell me what a typical week in your life is like.

- In what areas of your life do you need a partner to help you?

- What would you like to avoid in a relationship?

- What would you like to ask me?

How do I know if my date likes me?

- After your dates, your date contacts you to tell you how much they enjoyed it.

- There isn't a lot of time between dates.

- You sense in your date their excitement and joy of being with you.

How much should I reveal about important things about me? And when?

The answers are a judgment call on your part. Some people reveal things right away about their health, divorce, children, and past. Others hold back until they know they are interested in the other person.

Remember, you are in charge of you!

Should my partner and I move in together?

Research shows that living together works best when there is a serious talk about getting engaged — and then getting engaged and getting married within about six months to a year after getting engaged. Of course, there are always exceptions such as military service or health or family issues.

When should I introduce my new partner to my children and family?

Once again, it's your decision. Some people introduce their family and children right away to a new partner. But it's not recommended that your children spend lots of time with a partner whom you are not sure you want in your life.

Yes, some people say, "have them meet immediately!" But, think carefully about that choice. Your children — or family, for that matter — will probably be on their "best behavior" — and not give your potential partner an honest sense of your children and family!

Research shows that children don't deal well with a constantly changing cast of characters — meaning your dates and potential partners. The children wonder, for example: Should I care about this person — and then get attached — and then feel awful when they are gone? Should I be nice — obnoxious?

I advise being caring and cautious regarding your children's feelings. When you know that your new partner and you are most likely going to be a couple, then you can slowly introduce him or her to your family and children.

I hope all these ideas help you. Your head might be spinning now — but it's a good time to test and trust your instincts — and then see if you are correct. YOU MATTER!

Relating Better
With Your Partner

Hooray! YES! You found someone you like and love — and who likes and loves you! (Please note that I included the word "like.")

But there still are a few things that bother you.

Often, those things are about decisions you already made — and the decisions that need to be made about unresolved issues.

It might surprise you to learn that even mutually happy couples report that they have issues that have been unresolved for years!

Really? How could that be? The short answers are:

- Some decisions are just too hard to make

- Couples have strong fears about regretting some decisions

- They are not good at decision-making

- They usually end up getting angry, critical, and sarcastic when they try to resolve an issue.

- Some decisions are harder — or even impossible to "undo."

- For example, here are some questions that tend to be "either/or" issues:

- Should we have children?

- Should we adopt a child?

- Should we move to another city?

- Should we arrange to let a relative move in?

- Should we get married?

- Should we or one of us change careers?

- Should we or one of us go back to school for more training or education?

Whew! Now you can see how easy it is to let decisions remain unresolved! And just to complicate things a bit more, think about this finding from research in family and marriage:

The Problem-Solving Dilemma

- Mutually happy couples create a strong and emotionally healthy team by bringing complementary styles, priorities, and interests — BUT:

- It is these factors that also contribute them being on opposite sides of key decisions, such as the ones above, that cannot be easily made.

- As a result, even in the best of relationships, there are decisions that get "kicked around" forever.

But don't despair. Just knowing about this finding can calm your frustration. Before you learn about good problem-solving approaches, let's explore how you and your partner deal with disagreements and problem-solving.

QUIZ TIME!

Your Quick Diagnostic Problem-Solving Checklist

Read the following sentences .On a scale of 1-5, with 5 indicating the highest level of agreement to the statement, pick the number that best describes you and your situation. There is no score. The purpose of this checklist is to serve as a wakeup call. What did you learn? What would you like to improve — and how?

- My partner and I can solve problems without yelling or being sarcastic.

- We tend not to come to an agreement — and the issue remains unresolved.

- We respect each other's input.

- We hate big decisions.

- We have ways to decide.

- What did you learn about you?

The Most Common Not So Smart Ways to Settle Disagreements

- Blaming or Playing "You Said/I Did Not Say" Walking Away — or Storming Out

- Breaking or Throwing Things

- Caving In or Saying "Fine" — Even If You Disagree with Your Partner My Way or the Highway Approach

- Going Behind Your Partner's Back Brooding and Building Resentment

- Stopping Sex or Other Acts of Kindness and Connection

- Retaliating by Overspending, Drinking, Cheating, and Other Really Stupid Things Name-Calling

- Being Sarcastic

- Hiding the Checkbook

- Keeping "Score" of Who Got What They Wanted — or Didn't.

I don't think I need to explain why these tactics bring emotional damage — even if they bring some sort of truce. Marital research especially shows that walking away or using sarcasm and criticism corrode love. Which ones do you tend to use? Add your own.

And just what do couples fight the most about? Below is a list of the top issues and questions.

Hot Topic Questions and Issues

1. Money: Why do we fight about money?

Disagreements over money most often involve:

- Overspending

- Selfishness

- Lack of Shared Priorities

- Getting "Even" with Your Partner

But often the real issues include feeling valued, and/or having a "say" in the relationship decisions.

2. Each of Your In-laws: Why do in-laws have so much emotional power?

Disagreements about in-laws tend to be about:

- Whose Parents Get Preferential Treatment — so that You or Your Partner Can Finally Feel Loved by those Parents

- Disappointment and Anger over Failed Attempts of Your Partner to Manage Their Parents

- Feeling Controlled by Your or Your Partner's Family

But often the real issues include having your wishes and needs for your family honored, and seeing your partner become assertive with his family.

3. Your Children — and Your Partner's: Why Can't We All Get Along?

Disagreements about children tend to include:

- Different Styles of Parenting about the Rules of Who Disciplines Whom and How to Agree on Managing Children and Stepchildren

- Dealing with Your Exes

- Addressing all the Children's Acceptance, Criticism and Rejection of You or Your Partner — especially after a Divorce or Widowhood

But often the real issues include feeling empowered and "part of" the family, and developing a shared, team approach to childrearing.

4. Sex Issues or Relationship "Blahs": How Can I Keep Alive Feeling in Love?

Disagreements about sex and feeling that "spark" are usually about:

- Being Too Busy, Stressed to Take Time for You and Your Partner

- You or Your Partner Wants Sex More Frequently — Or You or Your Partner is Disappointed in the Sex You are Having!

- You or Your Partner Feel the Relationship is Stale or "In a Rut"

But often the real issues include "keeping that spark alive," feeling wanted, attractive, and special.

5. Your Friends — and Your Partner's Friends: How Do We Juggle Time and Closeness to Our Individual Friends?

Disagreements on friendships often revolve around:

- You or Your Partner Spends Too Much Time with Their Friends

- You or Your Partner Are Jealous or Mistrustful of Each Other's Friend of the Opposite Sex — Especially If You or Your Partner Confide Too Much in This Person

- You or Your Partner Doesn't Like Each Other's Friends

But often the real issues include feeling independent and free enough to make and keep your own life, and being able to enjoy doing things with each other's friends.

6. Vacations or Homes: How Can We Finally Resolve Where — and How We Live or Vacation?

Disagreements are often long-standing and unresolved about:

- Where to Go on a Vacation — and How Much to Spend and Who Should be Included

- You or Your Partner Either Wants to Move or Stay in Your Home

- Whose Money Gets Spent — and Who Has the Most Say in Decisions about Decorating, Moving, and Other Household Issues

But often the real issues include having equal "say" or fairness in decisions, and creating agreed upon memories and rituals.

7. Lack of Empathy and Respect from or for Your Partner: Why Can't My Partner Make Me Feel Loved and Understood?

Disagreements about lack of empathy and understanding usually happen because:

- You or Your Partner React First with Hostility

- You or Your Partner React First with Blame

- You or Your Partner Cannot Recognize His or Her Own Unkind Behavior

But often the real issues include:

- Feeling cherished and heard

- Actually liking your and your partner's behavior in the relationship

- Feeling that you made the right choice of partner.

8. Affairs and Other Trust-Busters: Can Our Relationship Heal — and then Thrive after a Betrayal?

About a third of couples cannot regroup over secrets and betrayals such as:

- Lies and Misuse of Money: Financial Infidelity

- Lies and Secrets about Affairs: Romantic Infidelity

- Lies and Secrets about Substance Abuse or Sexual Orientation

But often the real issues include wondering if you:

- Chose the right partner

- Can repair the hurt

- Face how much and how many of the "signs" you might have ignored or minimized.

9. Household and Family Management: Why can't my partner play a more active — or less dictatorial role?

Couples often have chronic struggles with the everyday family and household management such as:

- Lack of Reliability and Follow-through in You or Your Partner

- Feeling Burdened from Shouldering too Much Emotional Responsibility for the Relationship and Family

- Feeling Criticized and Controlled by Your Partner

But often the real issues include:

- Feeling undervalued and taken for granted

- Realizing that you and your partner really aren't a team "on the same page" of how you want to live.

Add Your Own Questions and Issues — and be sure to think about those underlying issues.

Now that you've had a chance to review some of the hot topics and questions, it's time for you to learn the Basic Problem-Solving Format.

No program can help you resolve every issue, but the Format has proven to be an extremely useful approach. But, like all new things, it takes time and a commitment to using them.

And what do we mean by time? Think in terms of seasons or six months — or maybe even a bit longer. Change is not easy. We are addicted to our habits of communication because:

- We feel familiar with them

- We are afraid of change

- We worry that this new style of communication might upset or challenge how we conduct our love relationships — and then risk revealing the limitation of it and ourselves and our partner

- We feel "loyal" to the beliefs and styles of our parents and caregivers — even if their ways are not so healthy

- We are afraid of our partner

- We are afraid of losing our partner

- We feel uncomfortable acting in new ways

- We worry that we can't do the steps in the Basic Problem-Solving Format.

Wow — no wonder change is so difficult. We all tend, over time, to "get comfortable with the uncomfortable" in our relationships. But, if you are truly hurting emotionally, then you will be far more motivated to use another approach. I recommend that you at least use this Format a few times to get used to it.

Basic Problem-Solving Format

The Basic Problem-Solving Format is just that — a method of handling many typical relationship challenges. But it is a general model that may not apply to dangerous situations such as domestic violence. If you are a victim of violence, consult one of your local organizations for help before you use this Format.

This Basic Problem-Solving Format is best used to activate your intuitive but often buried understanding of the problem and solution in "good enough" or "slightly off the track" relationships. It relies on empathy and care rather than complaint and criticism.

But before you look at the steps for the Basic Problem-Solving Format, you need to establish an intuitive understanding of each other.

How to Build an Intuitive Foundation about Each Other

Loving partners need to learn about each other's childhood "hot button topics." And be sure you recognize which disagreements activate your issues. Fights often occur because we are all Emotional Time Travelers, where the past infringes on the present. Most of us know how quickly our current disagreements drag the past into the discussion.

This problem-solving technique helps both of you become aware of the power of the past so that you and your partner feel that you "get" each other.

Don't you want a partner who "gets you?"

1. When a disagreement starts brewing — with no resolution in sight — stop the conversation immediately and use this format. If the timing is not right, agree to postpone the discussion to the next available time you have.

2. Regardless whether you talk now or later, make sure you know those "hot button issues" in you and your partner. They are often the "elephant in the room" that no one mentions.

3. I recommend creating a mental Drop Down Bar in your mind's eye. Think of those computer or website tabs that have drop down menus. Your Drop Down Bar should list the hot issues of you and your partner. Some typical examples are:

   • I'm always compared to my sibling

   • I'm the "outsider" because I am different

   • I'm always the first to be blamed for things— especially when it's the other person who is wrong

   • I never fit in my family

Write your thoughts about these:

Create a **Drop Down Bar** about:

YOU: My Hot Issues Are: _____

Create a **Drop Down Bar** about your:

PARTNER: My Partner's Hot Issues Are: _____

Now you are ready to use your understanding to solve your issues!

Basic Problem-Solving Format

1. Find a safe and quiet place to talk. If you or your partner tends to get heated, then go to a public place such as your favorite coffee shop.

2. Maintain loving, physical contact with each other. Hold hands. Or, let your legs touch.

3. Give up the idea that happy couples don't have disagreements. Happiness does not mean that you won't disagree. Your differences strengthen your relationship since couples tend to bring complementary viewpoints that can expand your thinking.

4. Report your feelings — don't be them. Give your partner a number from one to ten, with ten the highest, to indicate the importance of this issue to you. This signals your partner to talk now — or very soon.

5. Get mindful of your reactions. Use a "Do-Over" and a "Time Out" as soon as you know you misspoke or allowed a disagreement to escalate. We all make communication errors. They usually happen when you are stressed or the topic is one of your "hot buttons" or your partner's urgency or anxiety about needing closure makes you anxious or irritable. The fallout is a disagreement that gets way out of control.

6. Use the "Ask and Tell" technique. Couples can increase the ease of discussing issues when each person takes responsibility for telling their partner what is bothering them and asking their partner what is wrong when they sense their partner's mood.

7. Agree ahead of time that each of you will raise your hand like a Stop Sign to signal "Stop, take a breath, think about your words and tone."

8. Heed the rule that if you veto an idea or solution, you then must offer an option.

9. Instead of discussing an issue from your point of view, adopt your partner's point of view. All the above steps are important because they create a mindset of teamwork.

10. Talk out loud with your partner as though you are him or her. When you know your partner's issues, hot buttons, and past, then your empathy and understanding create a calmer and less defensive atmosphere.

An Example for Using the Basic Problem-Solving Format: Using the Pretending You are Your Partner Approach

In the beginning, this extremely powerful approach will feel uncomfortable. Let's use choosing a vacation as an example. You might lapse into saying something like: "You like to go to inclusive resorts where you can just plop yourself."

Instead, say: "I like to go one place and not worry about where to go, what to do or worry if I'm driving in the right direction."

Do you see what just happened in the example in the above paragraph? **Your ability to speak as your partner produced your understanding of your partner's needs.**

Of course, always stop to check with your partner if you are getting his or her issues and preferences correct.

So, let's say that your partner says you are on the right track. Now address why you-as-your- partner speaking has this preference to plop and stay put at an all-inclusive resort.

You might say something like: "My parents always fought in the car about getting lost and where to go to eat. It wasn't fun, and many times we drove around and around and came back to this lone hotel that didn't even have a snack bar. So, I feel instantly relaxed at a place that has everything."

Now, switch roles where your partner talks as you.

Your partner might say: "My family always 'cheaped out.' We

stayed at the worst places ever, and then we drove up and down the highway in search of a place to eat. I did learn, though, to turn it into something positive such as seeing new places. And now I like to take daytrips so I can see more. I don't like staying in one place."

After you tell your partner if he or she is on the right track your discussion will tend organically to lead to a solution that addresses both your needs.

In other words, the process itself, combined with your mutual display of empathy, will uncover the solution.

This example came from a real couple. They decided to stay at a resort in an area that had interesting daytrips that were nearby and not hard to get to. They splurged on the one that interested them the most, and, since it was far, they hired the hotel driver to take them there.

Use these steps — especially this last one — and your relationship will be stronger, happier, and more intuitive.

Signs Of A Good And Bad Relationship

Many of us imagine not wanting to admit this truth, but sometimes there are unhappy times even in the best of relationships. We aren't sure if we are in a relationship that is good or bad for us. We wonder what happiness looks and feels like.

And when we do experience loneliness, disappointment, and doubt, we don't know whether to trust our intuitive evaluation. This chapter will train your intuitive judgment about your intimate relationship.

For starters, here are two lists that you can use to tease out what you most likely already know about healthy and unhealthy interactions and partners. You have probably already observed these behaviors and wondered if they are signs that your relationship might need a tuneup.

Training your intuition is based on increasing your awareness, knowledge, and trust in your unique answers and explanations that are waiting for you and that are resting just beneath your fears of facing you!

The items in this list apply to both you and your partner.

Unhealthy Behavior Signs:

Each letter in **SMART** stands for:

S - Slights:

- Does your style of interacting include unkind remarks?

- Do you or your partner defend or not apologize or deny or dismiss this unkind behavior?

- Do you or your partner snipe at each other to express unhappiness?

- Do you or your partner have difficulty "going with the flow" and get nasty instead when small issues arise such as being a few minutes late or overcooking the vegetables?

M - Master Behavior:

- Do you or your partner react almost instantly with anger?

- Does one or both of you feel so deeply hurt that you can't even talk?

- Do important things get put off?

- Do you or partner rely on food, drugs, alcohol, spending or sleeping to manage fears and doubts?

- Are bickering and picking on each other the typical ways you deal with unhappiness and concerns?

- Do you or your partner avoid those "hot topics" out of fear of starting World War III?

- Do you, as a couple, have limited success in changing your unproductive actions?

- You can evaluate the degree of unhappiness and unhealthy behavior by observing if there is a sustained or increased level of:

- Frequency of various withdrawal and procrastination behaviors and outbursts, including verbal, physical, sexual, and financial abuse

- Intensity of reactions, including all the above

- Duration of reactions, including all the above

R - Ridicule:

- Do you or your partner make nasty fun of each other when one of you brings up issues?

- Do you make not-so-nice-fun of the other person in public?

- Do you or your partner forget or dismiss the other person's birthday and other celebrations — or celebrate begrudgingly without warmth and genuine enthusiasm?

- Do you or your partner call each other names or make nasty remarks under your breath?

- Does one of you make faces or turn away, throw your hands in the air or generally ignore conversations or walk out of the room — especially if the topic is important?

T - Trust Violations:

QUIZ TIME!

Select the word that best describes how much you worry or feel that your or your partner could:

1. Abuse the finances by doing things such as gambling, "borrowing" without paying back or buying expensive items without discussing it

☐ Always   ☐ Frequently

☐ Sometimes   ☐ Rarely Ever

2. Cheat

☐ Always   ☐ Frequently

☐ Sometimes   ☐ Rarely Ever

3. Lie or hide important information

☐ Always   ☐ Frequently

☐ Sometimes   ☐ Rarely Ever

4. Spend hours watching pornography

☐ Always   ☐ Frequently

☐ Sometimes   ☐ Rarely Ever

5. Get violent or sexually abusive

☐ Always   ☐ Frequently

☐ Sometimes   ☐ Rarely Ever

6. Hurt the children

☐ Always   ☐ Frequently

☐ Sometimes   ☐ Rarely Ever

7. Make you or your partner feel bad about you

☐ Always   ☐ Frequently

☐ Sometimes   ☐ Rarely Ever

8. Use drugs or alcohol

☐ Always   ☐ Frequently

☐ Sometimes   ☐ Rarely Ever

What are you learning about you and your partner?

Now let's look in the next section about healthy relationships!

You in a Healthy Relationship:

It's also a good idea for you to have some overall tips and reminders about what your good behavior should look like in a relationship.

Each letter in SMART stands for:

S - Self-Knowledge & Self-Awareness:

You will need to know about the patterns of your past love choices. Notice I do not say something like "types of men or women." It is much more important to look at your interactions with your partner.

QUIZ TIME!

Read the statements below. Then select one of the choices that best describes the degree of frequency in your love behavior.

1. I tend to take charge of decisions.

☐ Always   ☐ Frequently

☐ Sometimes   ☐ Rarely Ever

2. I tend to go along with things — and speak up when it really matters.

☐ Always   ☐ Frequently

☐ Sometimes   ☐ Rarely Ever

3. My partner tends to defer to my choices, decisions or wishes.

☐ Always   ☐ Frequently
☐ Sometimes   ☐ Rarely Ever

4. I like having lots of time alone or doing my own thing in my love relationships.

☐ Always   ☐ Frequently
☐ Sometimes   ☐ Rarely Ever

5. My childhood past has taught me that my wishes or needs are not heard or valued.

☐ Always   ☐ Frequently
☐ Sometimes   ☐ Rarely Ever

6. My partner and I have trouble making decisions, so we end up postponing them.

☐ Always   ☐ Frequently
☐ Sometimes   ☐ Rarely Ever

7. I love being a homebody and spending time with just my partner.

☐ Always   ☐ Frequently
☐ Sometimes   ☐ Rarely Ever

8. My parents taught me, said to me or showed me in their relationship that people are like planets in their own orbit.

☐ Always   ☐ Frequently

☐ Sometimes   ☐ Rarely Ever

9. I am easy-going and have no trouble if my partner makes the major decisions.

☐ Always   ☐ Frequently

☐ Sometimes   ☐ Rarely Ever

10. My parents taught me, said to me or showed me in their relationship that people are happiest when they do things with each other, friends or with the family.

☐ Always   ☐ Frequently

☐ Sometimes   ☐ Rarely Ever

11. I tend to know how to make right decisions on my own in my love relationships.

☐ Always   ☐ Frequently

☐ Sometimes   ☐ Rarely Ever

12. I don't like leaving issues open-ended, so my partner and I work together on solutions.

☐ Always   ☐ Frequently

☐ Sometimes   ☐ Rarely Ever

13. My parents taught me, said to me or showed me in their relationship that there is usually a leader and a follower.

☐ Always   ☐ Frequently

☐ Sometimes   ☐ Rarely Ever

14. My parents taught me, said to me or showed me in their relationship that people just sort of exist together.

☐ Always   ☐ Frequently

☐ Sometimes   ☐ Rarely Ever

15. I think relationships work best when there is one person in charge of important decisions.

☐ Always   ☐ Frequently

☐ Sometimes   ☐ Rarely Ever

16. I don't mind if my partner and I don't spend lots of time apart — working or just doing our own thing.

☐ Always   ☐ Frequently

☐ Sometimes   ☐ Rarely Ever

17. Infrequent sex doesn't bother me — as long as we are happy and nice to each other.

☐ Always   ☐ Frequently

☐ Sometimes   ☐ Rarely Ever

18. I didn't get married or move in with my partner to be apart from each other if it's not necessary.

☐ Always   ☐ Frequently

☐ Sometimes   ☐ Rarely Ever

These statements measure the two main continuums of **Emotional Comfort Zones:**

Feeling Safe and Warm in Intimate Relationships

- Individual Time (Apart & Cooler Feelings) vs Time Together (Closeness & Warmer Feelings)

- Lots of Say (More Control) vs Having Less Say (Less Control)

There is no "right" place to be on the continuum. Every relationship finds its own movement. You might remember reading this information and seeing the chart below. I like to review it because it strengthens your understanding of you — and increases the chances that you can trust your intuition, decisions and judgment. Besides — no one likes flipping back through pages to find information and charts that are about the current discussion!

To evaluate your past and future relationships, it's important to understand and use the underlying structure of intimate relationships. I recommend making a copy of the chart which you will see at the end of this discussion so you can use it for many relationships.

Research discovered that people want to feel safe and warm in their intimate relationships. Even if you see yourself as a strong, capable, and independent person, you still have normal,human needs to feel safe and warm with your partner.

Warmth

Warmth is a measure of your closeness — actual physical closeness and your feelings of closeness whether you are physically near each other or not. For example, military service often separates couples physically — but it does not necessarily diminish their feelings of warmth and closeness. Warmth can also include hugs, kisses, and love-making. Warmth is shown on the chart as time together and time apart. Togetherness is warm. Time apart is cool.

Yet, being in a relationship that tends to one end or the other does not mean you have a problem. There are times when — even in very happy and healthy relationships — you need or want to be physically apart due to work and family issues. Or, you need to be extra close because of other issues such as tending to health needs.

The goal is to be in a relationship that offers flexibility because flexibility creates a strong team that can solve a wider range of issues.

So, if one of you is ill, for instance, the other person can focus more on you. There is no magic spot on the continuum that is right for everyone. Just use the continuum as a tool to learn about this aspect in your relationship.

In general, healthy couples instinctively know when they have been too close or too apart. They signal each other about moving to the other end of the continuum.

Couples say things to each other such as: "I was just going to mention going back to that place." Or: "And I wanted to take a drive there this weekend,too!"

When couples are inflexible or unable to navigate happily and fairly easily between the extremes of warm and together vs apart and cool, they tend to get stuck in pursuing each other and pulling away from each other and being unhappy. Like Dr. Doolittle's two-headed llama,these couples manage their problems, unhappiness, anger,and disappointment by facing and moving in opposite directions!

Safety

Feelings of safety with your partner measure your degree of trust and comfort in your relationship. Healthy, happy couples feel a sense of ease, contentment, and reliability.

But one couple's feeling of reliability differs from another couple's. Some partners establish that sense of reliability and safety by taking charge. These partners are the decision-makers. Or, at the other end of the continuum, a partner experiences feelings of reliability and safety by giving up their "say."

Dealing with decisions and responsibilities can vary in each relationship. Couples take on different tasks because they have different strengths and coping styles — the heart of what is meant by "opposites attract." It's amazing how many couples unconsciously or intuitively know to choose someone with complementary abilities.

It's usually a good thing so many relationships find a good "opposite" match. Think of your relationship as a ship or country. You wouldn't want everyone to be a cook or navigator!

In some relationships, however, these differences are at odds with others. Even when couples are good problem-solving teams, their different styles result in no decision at all. For instance, one partner might make decisions that he or she feels are logical and sensible, while the other partner relies more on emotions that offer personal meaning.

Research of long-term couples who report mutual satisfaction with each other reveals that they often must live with important unresolved issues.

Ironically, as I previously mentioned, these same differences that made them such an effective team also left them with years of unaddressed decisions. Here's a quick review of the most common topics that often remain unresolved:

- Go to college or graduate school

- Move to another city

- Arrange for a relative to move in

- Change jobs

- Make a large purchase

- Have a child — or another child

On the other hand, couples who cannot live with the lack of resolution often end up bickering, arguing, picking at each other, and jockeying for power. Often, one of the partners needs to be "right." Over time, the person who tends to give up his or her say ends up feeling alone, disrespected, and estranged. To remedy this imbalance the estranged person needs to speak up — but without blame.

Although there is no magic place to be on the safety continuum, the goal, again, is flexibility so that each couple can become reliable in certain situations. Smart organizations and companies recognize this principle as having depth.

Now you are ready to take a look at that chart. Think carefully about the patterns of your current and past relationships. Where would you place your mark to indicate your degree and style of safety and warmth?

It might help if you go back to your choices for each of the statements above. Where would you place your spot on the chart for each of the statements? You are now on your way to increasing your self-knowledge!

The "Bones" of Love

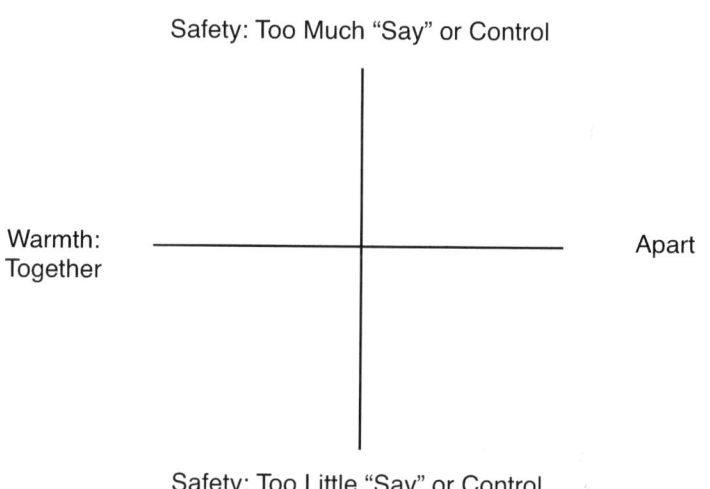

Safety: Too Much "Say" or Control

Warmth: Together — Apart

Safety: Too Little "Say" or Control

M - Mindfulness:

How aware are you of your feelings and physical reactions when you are with your partner? Your reactions are cues and clues about what's going on in you at the moment.

Read the statements below. Then select one of the choices that best describes the degree of frequency in your love relationship.

QUIZ TIME!

1. I am aware of my tone and choice of words — and how these factors contribute to my interactions with my partner.

☐ Always   ☐ Frequently

☐ Sometimes   ☐ Rarely Ever

2. I can't believe what "jumps" out of my mouth when I am upset with my partner.

☐ Always   ☐ Frequently

☐ Sometimes   ☐ Rarely Ever

3. It drives me nuts that my partner has a "knee-jerk" reaction to some issues or incidents.

☐ Always   ☐ Frequently

☐ Sometimes   ☐ Rarely Ever

4. I don't know why I react the way I do to certain issues or disagreements between us.

☐ Always   ☐ Frequently

☐ Sometimes   ☐ Rarely Ever

5. I can predict how my partner is going to react to certain issues or topics.

☐ Always   ☐ Frequently

☐ Sometimes   ☐ Rarely Ever

These seemingly simple questions are ways to "tease out" your Emotional Default Drive Style.

Just like a computer, you have emotional behavior that you automatically fall back on when your "hot button" gets pushed. And just how did you get these automatic reactions — good or bad?

Well, since you obviously were not "hatched" like a chicken, you most likely got these reactions from a mix of your genetics about your personality and your caregivers' behaviors toward you!

But here is the good news: You are not stuck with having to lead always with a dysfunctional Emotional Default Drive.

You can train your intuition, over time, to recognize these patterns in you and your partner — and use them to calm both of you.

For example, if your partner has a family history of being criticized, you might want to begin your conversations with statements such as:

- I am not picking on you or blaming you. Let's just find a solution together.

- I don't care how it started. What do you think we should do?

- I don't want either of us to handle this by avoiding, tuning out or arguing.

A - Anger Management and Anxiety Toleration:

Managing and recognizing your intense emotions are necessary for healthy interactions and healthy relationships. Even if you are angry at your partner, it's healthier and wiser to take these steps:

- Don't "warehouse" your feelings until they build up so much that your feelings rush out in anger.

- Instead, "report" your feelings rather than act hastily, abusively, or too defensively

- Signal your partner your degree of upset. Give your partner a number from 1 to 10, with 10 high, as to how much you are angry or hurt.

- Don't play "history" where you rehash every little word of what you think "He or She Said" vs "You Said." Anxiety tends to distort memory and tone.

- Play it forward and move quickly toward a shared resolution — including postponing it until a certain time.

However, if your partner is abusive, then I strongly recommend that you seek counseling first to discuss safe ways to express your feelings. Abusive partners often become more abusive when you speak up or threaten to leave.

R - Risk-Taking and Rebound Ability:

You must risk putting your heart out there for love. It is confusing that since the biggest fear of humans is to be abandoned physically and emotionally, we often hide the part of us that we find least lovable. Yet, if you want to feel loved, known, accepted, respected, and celebrated, you have no other choice.

Test your emotional risk-taking in this relationship and in general. Select the answer that best describes you.

QUIZ TIME!

1. I don't think I've really let my partner "know" me.

☐ Always   ☐ Frequently

☐ Sometimes   ☐ Rarely Ever

2. I respect my partner, so the problem of opening up is in me!

☐ Always   ☐ Frequently

☐ Sometimes   ☐ Rarely Ever

3. My partner does not "get" me.

☐ Always   ☐ Frequently

☐ Sometimes   ☐ Rarely Ever

4. My partner is a good role model for me, so, even though it is difficult, I tell my partner what's going on in me.

☐ Always   ☐ Frequently

☐ Sometimes   ☐ Rarely Ever

5. I have trouble "opening up."

☐ Always   ☐ Frequently

☐ Sometimes   ☐ Rarely Ever

6. I don't really know why my hot buttons get pushed — and that frightens me so much that I don't want to go "digging" inside me to find out about me.

☐ Always   ☐ Frequently

☐ Sometimes   ☐ Rarely Ever

7. My partner has a way of reacting that can be unkind or insensitive.

☐ Always   ☐ Frequently

☐ Sometimes   ☐ Rarely Ever

8. I like "The Me Who is Me" in this relationship.

☐ Always ☐ Frequently

☐ Sometimes ☐ Rarely Ever

9. We somehow end up yelling or walking away or storming out of disagreements.

☐ Always ☐ Frequently

☐ Sometimes ☐ Rarely Ever

10. It's not easy, but we are good problem-solvers who respect — and understand each other's differences and hot buttons.

☐ Always ☐ Frequently

☐ Sometimes ☐ Rarely Ever

T-Trust

Do you each trust that you can trust each other? It sounds like a circular question, but think about it. Believing and feeling that your partner is your "wing-man" or "wing-woman" is very important.

Select the answer that best describes your situation.

QUIZ TIME!

1. My partner is willing to compromise and place my needs first when necessary.

☐ Always   ☐ Frequently
☐ Sometimes   ☐ Rarely Ever

2. My partner and I act with integrity, sincerity, empathy, and maturity.

☐ Always   ☐ Frequently
☐ Sometimes   ☐ Rarely Ever

3. We both know that we can — and do — discuss anything — and with respect for each other's needs and opinions.

☐ Always   ☐ Frequently
☐ Sometimes   ☐ Rarely Ever

4. We share common values about fidelity, finances, family, and feelings.

☐ Always   ☐ Frequently
☐ Sometimes   ☐ Rarely Ever

5. We both feel "lucky" to have found each other — even if at times I would like friendly Martians to take him or her away for a few hours or days!

☐ Always   ☐ Frequently

☐ Sometimes   ☐ Rarely Ever

You will have accomplished this skill by becoming more intuitive about you, your partner, your relationship style, and each of your childhood histories.

On a separate piece of paper — or in the space below if you printed out these tips — write the things that have really "spoken" to you.

If you are unhappy in love, don't act in haste. Most of the time, you can wait to break up. If you feel your life and safety are in danger, seek counseling to develop a safety plan first before you pack your bags.

You can use these guides for each of your love relationships — past, present and future!

Finally, here is a checklist that you can use as a reference. Look at it often to remind you about loving relationships.

Relationship-Building Checklist

Can You Say You Have Built a House of Love?

Healthy relationships are built over time. Here's a building checklist that forms the foundation of a good love match! Think about each statement. Your goal is to say: "Yes, we have that!"

- We like each other for who we are — and aren't — in the relationship!

- I like how and who I am in the relationship.

- I like how and who my partner is in the relationship.

- We want each other to feel good, and we support each other's goals in life.

- We are independent and have our own interests.

- We see our own family and friends whenever we need or want–alone and with each other.

- We celebrate that we each have friends who may be different from our partner.

- We celebrate our differences — and we know that we can learn from each other.

- We value and help our partner with his or her family relationships.

- We are good at listening and talking to each other — with love and kindness.

- We have different opinions and sometimes disagree — but we listen to each other and develop wise decisions and compromises — big and small. For example, we take turns deciding what movie to watch!

- We can tell each other truthfully what we think and what we want without being afraid of being hurt or put down.

- We don't use sarcasm or criticism to express our points and feelings.

- We trust the other person to be honest.

- Sexual intimacy is what we both want — and no one is pressured into it. We can be honest with each other about what we like/don't like.

- If there is jealousy, we listen to each other, talk about it, and try to work things out together (instead of making threats or demands that restrict the other person's freedom).

- We both respect the other person's right to have their own private communication with their friends and family.

Creating and sustaining love takes time, empathy, relationship skills, and self-honesty.

Breakups

From my research I learned that the two most challenging issues about breakups are:

- Inability to trust your love judgment and be open to dating

- Doubting your ability to recover and move on after breakups

In some ways, these two issues are the opposite side of the same coin:

- If you can't trust your love decisions, then you close down your openness and receptivity to falling in love again. This choice makes you "rusty" at reading your reactions to potential partners, and it prevents you from developing your ability to assess accurately your dates. Even worse, it reinforces your belief in yourself that you can't trust your love instincts — and that perhaps "there is something wrong with you."

- If you focus more on the "rotten-ness" and "wrong-ness" of your ex-partner, you risk avoiding the agonizing but necessary work of psychological self-examination. By limiting your self-knowledge you leave yourself vulnerable to making more love missteps.

Now imagine that this coin is made up of varying strengths of fear of loneliness. The thicker the coin, the more you fear being alone — and the more likely your fears will lead you to grab the next "sorta," okay-enough person when life events such as illness or job loss make you feel more vulnerable.

This chapter will help you to train your breakup intuition so you can choose more wisely the next time. Here are the most common questions and issues from our research.

1. How Do I Know If I Am NOT Handling My Breakup Well?

If you experience the items on the list below for more than two weeks, I recommend you see a counselor. And why not?

It is not a good idea to volunteer to close doors that can open to you and your happiness — even if these doors lead you through some anxiety for a while. You have far more to lose by not getting some guidance and tips. Invest in you! You are worth it. You will learn to build the emotional confidence and bravery you will need to remain open to your correct intuitive signals!

Breakup Recovery Checklist

1. Which statements describe you?

Read each statement out loud. Read them again out loud. Pay attention to which ones give you a reaction such as:

- A roll in your stomach

- A flutter in your heart

- A nod of your head

- A wave of nausea

- A rush of anxiety

- An "Aha" moment

- A Chill

- Any other sensation or thought.

Read the statements below out loud twice.

A. My appetite has really changed. I'm either eating too much or too little.

B. I find myself relying on drugs or alcohol to make me feel better.

C. I have trouble falling asleep or staying asleep.

D. I've lost interest in the things that I normally do.

E. I can't concentrate or motivate myself at work or school.

F. I can't stop thinking about this person who is no longer in my life. I wonder if there is anew person in their life already.

G. I've been contacting my ex and leaving mean messages or

stalking them or damaging my ex's property, and basically making their life miserable.

H. I cry a lot.

I. I tell anyone who will listen about this breakup.

J. I have lots of aches and pains or headaches or stomach upsets.

K. It feels like my life is over.

L. I don't feel like being around my friends and family.

M. I don't have a lot of energy, and I've stopped exercising or doing things that made me feel good.

N. I don't think my life is worth living much longer, and I think of how I could end it and stop this pain.

All these items are important. But if items A, B, H, K, M or N created a reaction in you, seek help right away. Do not minimize your reactions.

Say out loud twice:

My feelings count
I matter—and I will shine

Let's start with a short quiz. I don't create scores for most of our quizzes. Instead, the purpose of them is to help you recognize your patterns.

Is it Love — or Rebound? Quiz

Select the answer that best describes your thoughts, feelings or actions.

1. Fairly soon after this or other breakups, I really think I found the right person this time!

☐ Always   ☐ Frequently

☐ Sometimes   ☐ Rarely Ever

2. I get shocked and disappointed that the new person ends up disappointing me, too.

☐ Always   ☐ Frequently

☐ Sometimes   ☐ Rarely Ever

3. I tend to choose someone who seems "totally opposite" from my previous partners.

☐ Always   ☐ Frequently

☐ Sometimes   ☐ Rarely Ever

Now let's see why these questions are important. Oh — and please keep in mind that the following discussion and tips take time to master — so don't worry if you stumble. Just get started!

1. Let's start with the first statement — which has to do with *loneliness and anxiety.* Of course, fate can favor you, and so you really can find someone very soon who is a good choice. But if your tendency is to get into another intimate relationship quickly after a breakup, you just might be tempting that fate.

Even if you are sure that you are over your recent break up, be careful about falling in love too soon again. How do you know if your new love is a wise choice?

Get mindful of your behavior in your new relationship. Put on an imaginary pair of glasses that allow you to be present and to observe your actions at the same time. Throughout your new relationship keep a journal and make sure you include commenting on these general questions:

- Am I acting out of fear of being alone?

- Am I rushing sex to "seal the deal?"

- Am I really happy?

2. The second statement addresses acting in haste to avoid feeling your doubts about whether you are lovable. Ask yourself these questions. I recommend keeping a journal.

- Am I taking charge of the relationship out of fear that he or she will leave?

- Do I accept unacceptable behavior from my new partner out of fear that he or she will leave me?

- Am I feeling "high" on finding someone so soon?

Don't waste your energy by hiding from the emotional pain of facing you. And it's never wise to hold on for dear life to a relationship that is not good for you.

3. The third statement is about the tendency to over-correct your previous unwise choice. For example, if you chose a partner who was too mild, you might look for someone who takes over. Ask yourself:

- Do I have a "say" in this relationship? And does my partner have a "say?" Or, have I over- shot my previous relationship by choosing someone who is way too opposite? It's very easy to believe — and feel — we have made a wise love choice because they are so very different from our last relationship. Be careful about choosing anyone who has too much or too little "say or voice or choice" in the relationship—including YOU!

- Do I feel that we are each other's trusted "wing-person?" In other words, do I trust this person to be capable and reliable?

- Do do I feel suffocated or ignored? Needy partners can use you up. You get exhausted from doing way too much — even though at first you thought your new strategy should be to take charge! Ironically, a seemingly warm and attentive person can actually make you feel that you and your needs are ignored — because you are so busy taking charge that your new partner does not think you actually need anything!

Don't focus so much on the "type" of person." Pay more attention to how you interact.

This concept of over-correcting your previous love choice can trap you in a Flip Cycle of Love. It's such an easy — and unwise — rut. And most of us have been caught in it.

This love misstep is so important that I repeat this chart that has appeared in other chapters. After all, you might have turned to this chapter first! And if you have already applied this chart, see what else you are learning about you!

Being Aware of Getting Stuck in The Love Flip Cycle: It Can Trap You in Failed Attempts and Rebound Love!

It's easy to get stuck in a Flip Cycle and Rebound Love Patterns. You hope someone very different is the solution. For example, let's say you tend to be attracted to someone who seems to be a successful and charismatic leader. You like his or her confidence and success. But, oh no, you misread this appeal. This person actually wants to control too much.

So, you break up finally, and you vow to choose someone who has a mild manner. Yet, later you discover that this partner often can't be decisive. In addition, they tend to want to be with only you —

and they can make you feel that the relationship is choking you around your neck!

So, you over-correct again and you choose someone whose pattern is to take charge of life — and then of you go back and forth — and back and forth!

But notice that these examples are just upside-down versions of the same pattern where someone is either too much or too little in charge or too passive — or too distant or too clingy.

The healthiest relationships consist of partners who fill in the gaps for the other partner's weaknesses and who can offer flexibility.

Here is a slightly revised version of the chart about love patterns that can serve as a quick diagnostic tool for your intimate relationship. Think of it as being similar to one of those tire pressure hoses that checks whether your tires are strong or weak, or flat or too full.

Look at the ends, and the top and bottom of the chart. Where would you place your old — and new — relationships? Be wary of the rebound relationship that you might have gotten into too quickly. Often, these new relationships are failed attempts to fix what you thought was so wrong about your previous relationship.

It's too easy to over-correct your choice of new partner.

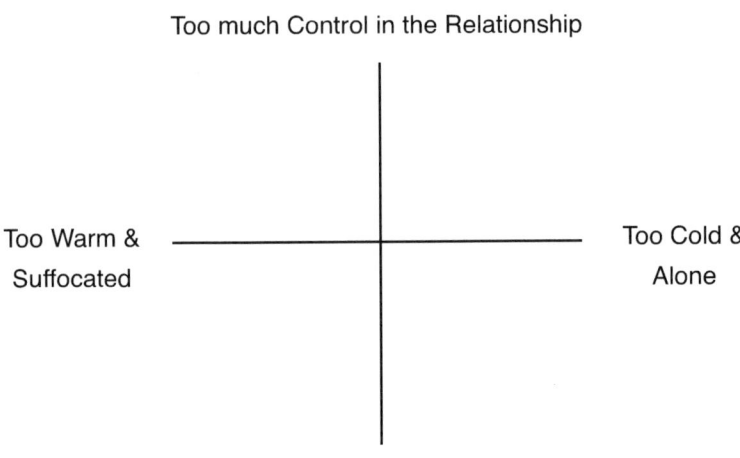

Too much Control in the Relationship

Too Warm & Suffocated

Too Cold & Alone

Too Little Say or Input in the Relationship

2. How Do I Move on After a Break up?

Maybe it is good that you aren't with so-and-so any longer. But, still, it hurts — and confuses you. Every situation has different details, but here are the top things to consider that emerged from my research and work with thousands of women. Here is a re-fresher checklist.

My Moving On Checklist Statements of Things I Can Say About Me

1. I did not swear off love for a longtime.

2. I toughed — or am toughing out--my sadness and confusion.

3. I really am committed to learning about me.

4. I am not rushing into another relationship.

5. I do not think I am unlovable.

6. I accept that I chose unwisely — but I am not "beating myself up" about it.

7. I am not hiding out from life or love.

8. I am not having sex with just anybody in order to feel alive or wanted.

9. I am not choosing someone just to prove I can attract someone.

10. I am not fooling myself by working long hours to fill my life.

11. I am not fooling myself by closing up my heart and believing that "if love is meant to be, it will just happen."

12. I am not managing my emotional pain by over-eating or other unwise behavior.

3. What are the Top Questions I Should Ask Myself about My Relationship History so that I Can Really and Finally Learn about Me?

No one likes making the same mistake too many times. Yet, you are seeing how easy it is to get fooled in love. You choose this "type" of person and then another "type" and you end up even more unhappy and confused.

And when you read books, you are often given either quick platitudes such as "don't date a moocher or controller" or you are given primarily big issues to think about such as respect and shared values.

And then you get shocked and disappointed again because you did choose someone with your values — and just look how that turned out.

By now, I hope you can see that I don't support focusing on "types" of partners. Instead, YOU are the focus of you! And, yes, I do support big issues such as shared values — but I also provide you with a different way of seeing how you might use your values. For example, as you are probably already learning, you might choose someone who thinks just like you—and then doesn't add anything to creating a team that can solve problems in varied ways.

Here are some questions to help you understand your past relationship. But I warn you: These are hefty questions that require more than one time to think about them. I recommend writing down your thoughts in a journal — and then revisit and revise your answers.

Smart Questions to Ask YOU

- Why did I choose this person? What do I think went wrong?

- What was going on in my life when I chose this person? What qualities do I now know I need in a relationship?

- Why do I end up creating the same kinds of problems I had in other relationships? What influence did my parents and childhood have over my love problems now?

The Importance of Your Emotional Default Drive

As I have mentioned many, many times already in other chapters, we all have Emotional Default Drives that quietly make us fall back on old relationship styles and love attractions. It originates in our upbringing.

This Drive can seem to cast a spell on you. It can trick you into feeling "chemistry" for an unwise partner choice. Eventually, you wonder: What's wrong with me? Why can't I be happy in love?

There's probably nothing wrong with you! We humans like to feel emotionally comfortable. But, oops — what makes you feel this sense of comfort can often come from what you learned about love, trust, closeness, control and too much accommodation from your caregivers.

If their lessons in love and life are not healthy, then you must unhook you from these lessons. And that unhooking can temporarily make you feel anxious and "not you." You must be able to recognize your family's way of dealing with the issues above, as well as anger, stress, respect, conflict and fears.

And even if you don't like how your family and caregivers managed these factors, you still might find yourself unknowingly incorporating — or even reproducing — these ways in your love relationships.

Detecting and avoiding falling back on what you learned from your family's own Emotional Default Drive are not easy tasks. But look at the word "learned" in the previous sentence. If you learned them, then you can *unlearn* them.

Unlearning and developing new ways of managing all the issues above require you to tolerate feeling *uncomfortable and disloyal* to your family until you replace your old Emotional Default Drive with a new and healthy feeling of comfort and new, accurate "chemistry."

Over time, you will learn to be suspicious of your feelings of emotional comfort. You will be able instantly to "run through" your unique questions about you in love!

For example, you might say to yourself: " I am attracted to this exciting but volatile and controlling person because I was used to dealing with a parent who chose a mate like this. Now am I attracted to this new person and not realize that once again I might find myself as a second class citizen to a charismatic but often disrespectful person?"

My research shows that knowing your Emotional Default Drive and being able to withstand changing your Comfort with a Dysfunctional Comfort Zone are the secrets to making a wise match.

The **Foundations** chapter offers more exercises and discusses other aspects of your Emotional Default Drive. I strongly recommend that you get as familiar and skilled as possible in dealing with this key issue.

Here are some sample questions to "run through" in your mind:

- Who in my family could not be alone?

- Who in my family cannot withstand emotional self-examination?

- What did my family teach or show me about dealing with anxiety?

- What did my family show me about dealing with people who control? Or people who give in? Which person am I? And do I like that about me?

4. How Do I Become an Expert in My Intuitive Reactions, Feelings, and Assessments While on Dates or in New Relationships?

Observe you on a date and your date at the same time. Observe important cues from your date. Take a look at the **Reading People** chapter for more details. Here are the top things to observe and do:

- How does my date treat the wait staff?

- Does my date listen or talk only about him or her?

- Does my date "charm" me too much and make me feel too "special?" These could be signs of this person reading your vulnerability — and then taking advantage of you.

- Observe your own levels of too much excitement and anticipation for a date with this particular person. This reaction could be a sign that you are so excited that you might overlook your date's important shortcomings.

- Go to the restroom and check your pulse. Ask yourself: Is my pulse racing because I am falling in love too quickly? Is my pulse racing because I am uncomfortable with a person who is actually good for me — but who also defies my old patterns and family history?

• Read books about reading people.

5. How Do I Change the Goal of Dating from "Finding the One" to "Testing the Accuracy of My People-Reading Skills?""

Date lots of people. Don't worry if the person doesn't seem your "type" or if there isn't any "chemistry." You might be surprised. Give "second chances" so you can confirm or change your view of someone.

And be sure to not to give in to your frustration of not finding "The One" — and therefore stop dating!

Overriding this pessimism prevents you from hiding out and swearing off love. If you don't override your frustration, you risk getting caught in a terrible cycle:

Your "down on love" mindset and love avoidance perpetuates a low evaluation of you And then this low sense of self-worth makes you avoid love opportunities

Remember this Drill-Down Chart below as a reminder of what might be your unwise way that could be lurking at the core of your fears.

My Drill-Down Chart to Avoid Hiding Out from Love

- I swear off love

- Because I don't want any more hurt

- Because I believe I can't tolerate the pain of rejection and confusion Because I doubt that I can recover from those feelings

- Because I believe these feelings are proof that I am deeply flawed and unlovable.

The result of fostering this Drill makes you choose unwisely again because you get caught in another love trap. Remind yourself of this next list.

The Who Do I Think I Am Anyway Love Trap

- I am flawed

- So who am I to judge others?

- Therefore I shouldn't rule out potential partners

- So I end up with another partner who isn't good for me And I should tolerate their behavior

- Because I am flawed, too.

6. After a Breakup How Do I Stop from Going Back to This Same Style of Bad Relationship Pattern and Choice? OR: Even Go Back to the SAME PERSON?

Yes, it certainly can be tempting to go back to a bad relationship. You think: The person has changed. And I've changed. And who am I to judge?

> Your best preventive medicine for going back to a bad relationship is to withstand your sadness, self-knowledge, anxiety and loneliness.

Your smart thoughts may tell you: "I did the right thing," but your feelings can hijack your decisions. At night or during those ill-timed pangs of loss you feel the urge to call, email, text or run over to your ex's place to drop off that one thing of his or hers. Perhaps a letter, you think? Yes, that's it. A long letter outlining what went wrong — in the hope that your words will jump-start a miraculous change in your newly-dumped partner.

Whoa! Wrong moves! Deal-breaker break ups are just that — incidents that made you decide to end your relationship in the first place! Yet, a dangerous mix of doubt about your good-bye lures you to try again. If you have broken off a bad relationship, use the guide below that has top questions to help you.

Tough Questions to Ask You about Going Back

What makes me want to go back?

Doubt and loss are the two main culprits that conspire to make you regret your break up. At first, you feel justified. You feel strong, determined. You think you've arrived at that fork in the road and that now there is no turning back.

Usually, breakups occur at decisive moments that you can't ignore. Perhaps they broke your jaw this time. Or, you discover concrete proof that your partner cheated on you or took your money. Your outrage and hurt reach an intensity that provokes a break up. You know you did the right thing.

It's the *staying* with your decision that is now the surprising hard part. Soon, doubt can set in. You wonder: Did I give my partner a fair chance? Shouldn't I forgive? Who am I to judge another? And shouldn't I take into consideration that my partner had a bad childhood — but really truly is trying?

Along with the doubts are your feelings of loneliness. It's not so easy being over forty or being a single parent or living on one salary. Maybe going back isn't such a bad idea, you think. After all, you've already logged in years with this person. Wouldn't it be a waste of time to try to meet someone else?

All these reactions sound logical, but they are not. They are your fears talking.

What should I do when I want to act on these fears?

Review your relationship facts. Most likely, in your bad relationship you put up with things you shouldn't have or you minimized differences that are important to you.

Do the "Crumb Inventory." Write in a journal all the incidents that made you feel hurt. Don't disqualify *any* of them. The tendency of partners is to minimize potential deal-breakers or to "let slide" differences and issues that must be addressed sooner than later. Ageing, loneliness, financial concerns, low self-esteem, and protecting the years of your emotional investment can lead you to accepting crumbs — or, even worse, mistaking crumbs for cake!

But what should I do when my negative feelings are just too much?

Sometimes feelings can be so intense that they overwhelm and frighten you. They also make you feel wrong, inadequate and undeserving. Here are some tips that have worked.

A. Keep a Negative-Corrections Self-Thoughts Journal. Make two columns. Create one column called **Negative Thoughts**. In that column write one negative thought about you on one line.

Add another thought below it and keep adding one negative thought per line.

Label another column **Corrections**. In this column write your positive thoughts for each negative thought.

When you counteract your negative thoughts about yourself, you are building new coping skills.

B. Keep a Success of Bad Times List of all the things you've overcome. Review, for example, all the things you did to manage illness, loss of a loved one, job, house or pet. When you remind yourself of how you got through hard times, you can more easily activate your positive thoughts and pro-active behaviors.

C. Stand in Front of the Love Judge exercise. Pretend you are in a Court of Love. You must plead your case about how you should be treated with leniency. Tell the Judge about how you tried, what you learned, what you ignored and why. What would the Judge rule?

7. Why is it so Hard for Me to Get Over Short-Term Relationship Break Up?

Don't think you're being weak if you have trouble recovering from a short-term relationship break up. These break ups can hurt in different but important ways.

People most likely offer you sympathy when your long-term relationship ends. Few know why or how the short-term ones hurt so much, too. Here are the top discussions about why you might be feeling hurt and anger when these briefer love connections fall apart.

These relationships are often more intense and passionate. Falling for someone so quickly can seem as though you're riding a roller-coaster. You feel the mixed thrill of anticipation, speed, and the unexpected. You have high hopes, get that rush of hormones that trick you into feeling "chemistry," and you earnestly believe you've finally found The Right One. But the higher you climb, the farther you have to fall. The emotional crash from the break up can really hurt.

Since you didn't have enough time to create a pitted past of arguments and long-standing, unresolved issues, you really experience the rejection deeply. You feel cheated because the person seemed to reject you before you had a chance to be "known" and valued. You want to send that person one more message that says: "You weren't fair to me. You judged too soon." You are left holding the negative bag of thoughts with sentences such as "If I've been turned down before they knew my very private issues, then I must really not be very acceptable."

What makes recovery so painful is that finding someone who "feels" right is not easy, and when that special someone calls it quits, it seems that the number of Right One's has shrunk. Since most of these intense relationships involve sex, you feel both physically and emotionally exposed.

Here are some ways to heal from this kind of rejection.

How to Speed Your Recovery

A. Place this sentence in your cell phone and on pieces of paper in your work desk and near your home phones:

"This person didn't really get to know me, so I have not necessarily been rejected for my true and whole self."

In private, say these words out loud whenever you start being too hard on yourself. Take a bathroom break at work, for example, and whisper these words in the stall!

Do the same thing with these sentences:

"I might have seen this person as a good match, but this partner might not have seen me as a good one for them. But people often don't know their needs and issues."

B. Since it's possible that you could have contributed to this false impression of you, ask yourself these questions:

"If I could have a "do-over," what would I do differently?" How might this person have gotten a wrong sense of me?" For instance, did you get drunk? Get clingy, too sarcastic or remote? Did you complain or criticize?

If you think there is still a chance with this person, write and snail-mail a note (no emails or text messages!). Your note could say something like:

"I think you got a false impression of me." (You might want to describe what might have prompted this impression.) *"I was going through some truly difficult times."* (You could mention briefly what it was that you were experiencing.) *"Even if you don't want to date, I hope we can be friends. Perhaps I can do something for you."* (Offer a favor such as giving the person a contact that you talked about).

B. If all else fails, get through your need for closure. Unfinished business or being "misread" can gnaw away at you so much that you might be tempted to "try one more time" to explain things and re-connect. Resist this urge. Better strategies are to keep a journal, confide in someone or seek therapy. You can move on!

8. How Do I Handle The One I Left After A Breakup?

Yes — you broke up because it wasn't working. Every relationship has unique details about unhappiness. You may still harbor some doubts, but, for now at least, breaking up feels like the right thing to do.

It wasn't easy — regardless if the relationship was very bad or just not a good match with a person who was good!

You may already know that your next steps after you close that door on this relationship are to: Learn about you and this relationship

Move on with your life and be open to love again.

But — oops! You still might be left with the question: *How do I deal with the person I just broke up with?*

Here are some tested answers to your top questions about handling the person you left.

Best Answers to your Top 3 Questions about Dealing with the One You Left

A. What do I say to this person if I don't know for sure why I brokeup?

Often, relationships don't seem to end for concrete or clear reasons. For example, you have no grounds to say things such as: They beat me. They cheated on me. They stole my money. They abused my kids.

Even if you were unhappy with your partner, you feel on shaky ground saying to yourself or others: "It just didn't work out."Or, "They weren't the right person for me."

If you don't know why you broke up, you might have difficulties explaining to your ex why you have to leave. They might call or text and ask you repeatedly: Why?

So what do you do? Here are some things you can say.

- I'm just not clear on what I want in life and love right now.

- I'm going through some rough times, and it's not fair for me to be with anyone until I take care of these things first.

- My work is so demanding and stressful that I know I can't give any relationship the time and effort and respect that I would like.

- It's not you — it's me. I have to sort out somethings.

- Our timing is off. I want this — and you want that.

- I just was not happy.

B. How much should I be in my ex's life after we've already broken up?

Sometimes, you and your ex can actually be friends. But be careful. Remember — you chose to break up with them! They may never totally reveal their hurt. I wish we could give you a magic answer that isn't too little or too much. Here are some thoughts and guidelines — not rules! Every relationship is different.

- Keep your breakup message clear. If they were abusive, we especially recommend keeping your distance and not engaging with your ex if possible. Abusers tend to over-respond to gestures of kindness and contact. They can interpret them as hope — and then get frustrated when you let them know that there isn't any.

- Don't rush to rescue your ex. We know — it's tempting to over-help those exes who are troubled or who just need a helping hand. If you really want to help them, let them experience life. You can't fix or rescue anyone. Pay attention to your guilt and its tendency to reel you back in to their life. For example, don't' send frequent texts to ask how they are doing.

- Don't put yourself in a compromising position where sex can easily happen. Sex with your ex can be a very selfish act. It sends mixed messages to your ex. Be kind. You wouldn't want someone to use you to feel close for the moment. So, keep your contact in public places.

C. When should I tell my ex that I am seriously involved with someone else?

It depends on the nature of your relationship to your ex. If you were smart and kind and did not send mixed messages, then you have probably already created a respectful emotional distance.

Here are some tips and thoughts.

You don't owe your ex your life story after your break up. No matter how much you are now friends, it's likely they harbor hurt and hope about you. Hold back on telling too much. You don't need to announce your new relationship status. If you do sense that your ex is in an emotionally strong place, you can give a general and brief statement.

Don't answer lots of questions about your new love. If they dig for details, that behavior might be a sign they are more hurt than you think.

Keep in mind that the seemingly nicest people can become violent when they think you have really moved on — without them! Don't flaunt or use your new relationship as a signal that you have truly moved on. It can re-engage you with your ex — or ignite their resentment. Your ex might interpret it as a sign that you are working too hard to get over them because you still feel an attachment toward them.

I hope this book helped you. Life and love are not always easy. No one gets through life without missteps. I don't use the term "Trial and Error."

Instead, get into a more productive mindset and use this term to describe your personal journey:

"Trial and Learn."

With Support, Cheer, and Best Wishes, LB

38774973R00087

Made in the USA
Middletown, DE
11 March 2019